A BASIS FOR MUSIC EDUCATION

A Basis for
Music Education

Keith Swanwick

NFER Publishing Company

TO MY COLLEAGUES AND STUDENTS

780·72

Published by the NFER Publishing Company Ltd.,
Darville House, 2 Oxford Road East,
Windsor, Berks. SL4 1DF
Registered Office: The Mere, Upton Park, Slough, Berks, SL1 2DQ
First published 1979
ISBN 0 85633 180 5

Typeset and Printed by
King, Thorne & Stace Ltd., School Road, Hove, Sussex, BN3 5JE
Distributed in the USA by Humanities Press Inc.,
Atlantic Highlands, New Jersey 07716 USA
Cover design by Pat Kattenhorn

Contents

Foreword

Artists as such do not need to talk or write in defence of their vocation as artists – though of course they do! Schoolteachers of the arts are in a very different position. In a world dominated, sometimes obsessed, by utilitarian needs, and the need to qualify for them by passing examinations, teachers of the arts are often forced into a defensive position; they have to fight for a place in the time-table, and too often must be content with the left-overs. 'How on earth,' a teacher of the visual arts, or dance, or music, may say to himself, 'am I going to convince "them" of the *importance* of what we are doing?' (A teacher of science does not have to face this problem.)

There is another question behind this. It is, 'How do I convince *me* that the work I am doing with my pupils is of real importance for their lives? If the subject happens to be music, it can be taken for granted – or one presumes that it can – that the teacher 'knows' for himself the importance of music, because he loves it. That is one thing: the justification for including music as a subject in the curriculum is quite another. This asks for a reasoned case, and it is essentially a difficult one to make out, since music, like other arts, has not anything like the same obvious usefulness as, say, geography or science, and it is difficult to get a message across to others who are not already sympathetic. This is particularly so if the teacher has not deliberately and explicitly worked out for himself conceptually the nature of music as an art and the functions and purpose of music education.

And this is something which teachers of music have, through no fault of their own, no particular qualification to do. For to articulate a *rationale* for music education requires some philosophical training; it is a branch of philosophy of education which includes aesthetics as an essential ingredient. Aesthetics as a branch of philosophy, with a few notable exceptions, received scandalously little attention in this country until after the Second World War, and it was not until the latter part of the sixties that it began to be applied academically to art education, though then it was only to a chosen few. So it is little wonder that the voluminous talk and writing about art education has consisted largely of the repetition of high-sounding words and phrases – 'self-expression', 'self-revelation', 'expression of the emotions', 'the education of the whole person', 'education for creativity' . . . and so on. I am not suggesting that there is nothing in such words and phrases, but only that the use of them for the most part sadly lacked disciplined clarity, and that the teaching of the arts has been adversely affected by their – sometimes pretentious – vagueness.

Here, at last, is a book for all music teachers. Its title is significant, *A Basis for Music Education*. It offers a *basis*, and a basis *for* music education. The basis involves a careful and clear examination and analysis of the fundamental concepts involved in music. What *is* music? Is music *meaningful*? It has no 'subject-matter' like literature; yet to call it 'meaningless', as Stravinsky said, seems absurd. What about 'stories' or 'messages' or speculations about the psychological states of composers? Is it self-expression, or expression of the emotions? Does the composer communicate by a code to his hearers? Is it the *form* of music which matters; if so what is the *content* of music? If music involves feeling and emotion, what have these to do with the feelings and emotions of life outside music? If music has its own 'meaning' in some sense, what is the relation of that to the different 'private' meanings different people seem to get out of the music? Does music refine our feelings and emotions? If so, how?

The asking of these questions (and many more), and the attempt to answer them – some of it necessarily speculative – is not just an exercise in analytic philosophy. The basic discussions in the first two chapters form a ground for a most interesting systematic *schema* for practical music education. By the invention of an ingenious mnemonic, three main items – Composition (including improvization, etc.), Audition (more than just 'hearing'), and Performance (C. A. P.) – are shown clearly as distinctions within the field of music education – as distinctions, but always in organic relation to one another. Another two, but subsidiary distinctions, Skill acquisition and Literature studies (including critical, historical and musicological writings) make up the picture; the final, total mnemonic, C.L.A.S.P., a rather pretty symbol of the unity-in-difference of the scheme. The last two chapters, on the often-heard battle cries – 'Creativity', 'Contemporary' and 'Integration' – and on Music, Society and the Individual, further exemplify the most valuable fruits of Professor Swanwick's fundamental thinking. Here is a delightfully written and illuminating book, and I am honoured in being asked to write this foreword to it.

Louis Arnaud Reid
(Professor-Emeritus of Philosophy of Education in the University of London)

ACKNOWLEDGEMENT

The quotation from MOVING INTO AQUARIUS by Michael Tippett are included by permission of the publisher: Routledge and Kegan Paul.

When I listen to someone else performing
my music it is clear the music has left
its creator and has a life of its own.
But the nub of the question remains . . .
'What does this music – or any music – do
within our present society, and what do I
think I am doing by composing it?'

MICHAEL TIPPETT (1974)
Moving Into Aquarius

Introduction

Music education seems to be passing through an interesting, if difficult period. Over a decade or so there has been a tremendous proliferation of ideas and suggestions in all branches of the profession. This is particularly noticeable at school level, where the comprehensive 'problem', the urban 'problem' and the creativity 'movement' have caused much soul-searching and re-appraisal of beliefs and strategies. But it is also noticeable among those teachers in higher education and even in instrumental teaching.

Music has always attracted the attention of philosophers and psychologists who find the phenomenon of music profoundly interesting and complex, an abstract yet powerful art raising all kinds of conceptual and experimental difficulties. More recently though, sociologists have turned their spotlight on music education, identifying 'élitism' in our professional practice, observing our narrow definitions of music confined to the Western 'classical' tradition and pointing out the inadequacies of our intellectual framework and teaching methodology. We are coming under fire.

It is not the purpose of this book to explore every highway and byway of music education, but rather to pick out those features that seem in greatest need of attention. Nor is it possible to specify in practical detail the answers to a multitude of various problems. Instead I am confining the issues to what I regard as central problems. The crux of it all seems to be that we badly lack any kind of conceptual framework. The consequences of this are twofold. In the first instance we miss a sense of direction in teaching, or indeed, may cheerfully take wrong directions. In the second place we are unable to look after ourselves when negotiating our way through the thickets of educational administration and politics, at whatever level in the system we may happen to be. Fundamentally we have no *rationale* that bears examination and stands up well against the views of different pressure groups. We have failed to notice and publicize the central core of music education, which is that music education is *aesthetic* education. The reason is not hard to see: we are busy people, practically involved with so much activity that time is not on our side. But we might also plead that the area of our concern is genuinely difficult to grasp and clarify.

My purpose here therefore, is to attempt to map out this central territory in a way that is general enough to be meaningful to teachers working in *any* musical setting but specific enough to motivate further thinking and development of practice in the field. This may seem ambitious. At the present time though, noting less will do.

Chapter 1:

The Meaningfulness of Music

Some teachers and musicians may regard the following discussion as a waste of time, and indeed, for some people it may be. Yet I would regard an exploration of this terrain as a fundamental and recurring challenge to any teacher of music who is more than a mere classroom 'operator'. Whether we are aware of it or not, we all hold assumptions about the nature of musical experience, its relative importance in human life, the ways in which it comes about and what kinds of activities are appropriate to promote it. Unexamined assumptions run very close to prejudice and are liable to be responsible for constricted views, unchanging attitudes, and bad professional practice. A really shaky assumption is likely to distort all that we do. Our ideas about music really matter. If, for example, we regard tonality as an essential part of music, then we rule out any possibility of *atonal* sounds being music, not to mention the music of other cultures where Western tonality does not seem to play much of a role. This will affect what we do as teachers, what music we select, what music we ignore, and how we approach it with our students.

Let us then take a few elementary definitions of music and see how well they serve us; the old one of music as 'organized sound' will start us off. A moment of reflection will show us that such a definition just will not do. Speech is organized sound, so is the noise of a road-drill or a telephone bell or a typewriter but we do not usually regard these sounds as music, though we might do so at times. Indeed, to consider these sounds as music would be to deprive them of their normal significance; we might attend to the 'music' of speech and not to what the person was saying, or we might contemplate the beauty of the telephone bell and never answer it. Of course music is 'organized sound' but is it not more than that? Would it be unfair to suggest that it is just this kind of definition that allows us to be satisfied with a class howling its way through the notes of a song or battering through endless and shapeless percussion salvoes? These activities may be organized but to many of us they may seem *unmusical*. Clearly then, it is possible to have organization of sounds without music, so something very important gets away when we use this particular definition.

Consider the definition that describes a musical sound as having regular vibrational characteristics as opposed to a noise with irregular sound-waves. A note on a flute then is musical while breaking glass is not. But what are we to make of the modern percussion section in the orchestra, or of recent compositions where glass is actually broken as part of a piece? It seems plain that there is here a confusion between music and pitch. Pitched sounds do have steady wave-forms but can we really regard all pitched sounds as music just because of that? Ambulance sirens, squealing brakes, squeaking doors and howling dogs make music whilst a tambourine does not, if we accept this definition. And, if the definition is accepted, a whole range of music is lost to us, including many contemporary developments. 'It has no tune', we protest, meaning only that its main features do not include successive steady pitched sounds relating to each other inside the tonal framework that we happen to have learned. Our definition prevents us from asking whether or not it might be possible to relate sounds in other ways, or whether turning our attention to timbre and texture instead of pitch variables might not be a valid way of making music.

Both of these definitions suffer from a fundamental failure to grasp an important distinction between what I wish to call 'materials' and what I call 'elements'. Let us consider some examples of these.

A pile of bricks is material: a wall is an element of a house.

A plank of wood is material: as a shelf in a cupboard it becomes an element of a piece of furniture.

A lump of clay is material: worked into a head-shape it becomes an element in a sculpted figure.

A series of notes making up a major scale is material: a phrase using some of these notes is musical element.

An electronic sound is material, so is a thud of a hand on a table: when related to other sounds and their own repetitions in time they become elemental.

The note 'A' sounding before a concert at the Royal Festival Hall is
musical material and a signal for people to take their seats: the
note 'A' that opens Wagner's *Rienzi Overture* is an element of that
particular piece of music.

An organ pipe sounding 'D' is to the organ-tuner raw material: to
the organist it is more likely to be part of a musical element, a bit
of a phrase or figuration, or a chordal sequence.

Looking more closely at these examples we might notice three
necessary conditions for musical materials to be transformed into
musical elements, or in other words, for sounds to become music.

1. *Selection:* Not every available sound is used; many are rejected
   and some are repeated a great deal.
2. *Relation:* The sounds are made to combine or to precede or
   follow each other in time.
3. *Intention:* The composer/performer intends to make music
   (whatever it is) and we intend to hear it.

Intention is of particular importance because as we can see in the
case of the organ pipe and the 'A' on the South Bank, the sound may
be the same or similar but we hear music or not depending on our
intention. In other words, the key to understanding what we mean by
a musical experience is to be found in psychological processes and not
in physical or acoustic measurements. It is, as they say, 'all in the
mind'; it all depends on our attitudes and previous experiences and no
machine that can measure sound organization or its relative regularity
is going to be able to tell us whether music is taking place or not. The
same sounds that might be music for one person may be nonsense for
someone else; it takes time to get into a musical style or into materials
of which we have had little or no previous experience.

Now if we can accept the distinction between materials and
elements we can begin to see things a little more clearly. We can
concede that any sounds might be musical material including
'collected sounds' on tape, electronically produced sounds, distorted
sounds, as well as traditional musical sound sources. We can also
acknowledge the stimulating effect of experimenting with sounds and
'discovering' them. Materials in themselves can be exciting things, at
least for a time. They also influence the development of music. The
huge spreading paragraphs of Bach's organ music are unthinkable
without the enormous mechanical lungs of the instrument itself. The
enlarged symphony orchestra seems absolutely right for Wagner as
does the array of electronic devices for Stockhausen: imagine either

confined to the string quartet. Instruments, new sounds, new techniques and inventions (for example the sustaining pedal on the piano) all help to fire the imagination of musicians but, and this is the point, by themselves they are sub-musical, or pre-musical. New sounds are not by themselves new music, and 'old' sound materials can still be fashioned into new elements. (When Schönberg said there was still plenty of music waiting to be written in the key of 'C' he was making the distinction between materials and elements). Nor are sounds as such, whether new or old, going to hold our interest for very long. How long can we sustain interest in sound as a phenomenon? How long can classes in school go about 'experimenting' with instruments, tape-recorded sound, or tearing up paper to make different sound-effects? The answer is, I think, for a little while only. The first thing is surely to enjoy working with materials of sound just as in pottery it is essential to have a good 'feel' of the clay at first, but the processes of selection, relation and intention must soon be brought to bear so that the making of music may begin. The same applies to an activity as 'traditional' as singing. Vocalizing the notes is one thing, it is a handling of materials; relating the sounds to each other to make phrases and lines and feelings of cadence is another, the sounds are then becoming elemental. With this distinction clearly in mind we can now consider more interesting and useful views of music.

One of the simplest views of the nature of musical experience was given long ago by the music historian Dr Burney (1726-1814) when he described music as an 'Innocent Luxury, unnecessary indeed to our Existence, but a great Improvement and Gratification to our sense of Hearing.' This is the notion of music as simply a pleasurable experience, and a very attractive view it is for it does not require elaboration and it can provide us with a simple way of evaluating our musical experiences. The more pleasure we get the better is the music. Taking this view would be to say that music is very like, say, taking a walk in the country or having a nice hot bath, relaxing, possibly stimulating, refreshing and so on. But although something of these pleasures may be a part of musical experience it would seem foolish to limit music to this kind of function. It really would not seem reasonable to suggest that the music of Beethoven or Boulez or even 'Genesis' is just an 'innocent luxury'. There seems to be something more substantial and 'gritty' in the experiences we derive from some of the music we hear and perform. Furthermore, it would seem that not everyone is able to appreciate the 'simple' pleasures of music when they are offered. Susanne Langer is very clear on this when talking about the arts in general:

'But now, since everybody can read, visit museums, and hear great music over the radio, the judgment of the masses on these things has become a reality, and has made it quite obvious that great art is not a direct sensuous pleasure. If it were, it would appeal – like cake or cocktails – to the untutored as well as to the cultured taste. This fact, together with the intrinsic "unpleasantness" of much contemporary art, would naturally weaken any theory that treated art as pure pleasure.' (Langer, 1942, 1951)[1]

It would appear that the pleasure view of music not only fails to account for some aspects of our musical experience but also excludes a good deal of the accepted repertoire.

A slightly more sophisticated view of music sees it as a form of play. 'This is more like it. When it really comes down to it music is purely and simply a game people play – or watch other people playing' (Geoffrey Brace, 1970).[2] This is a very old idea which can certainly be traced back at least as far as the Romans, who considered music to be a kind of arena sport, an opportunity for display and competition. The philosopher Schiller defines beauty as the 'object of the play impulse' and Herbert Spencer agrees. 'The activities we call play are united with the aesthetic activities'. And he goes on to say that just as the arts occupy the leisure part of life, so should they occupy the leisure part of education' (1911).[3] Notice here how a particular view of the arts gives rise to educational implications. As I said earlier, our assumptions about music matter and they affect how we deal with it in schools and elsewhere. Now of course there is much to be said for the play theory. If it takes some of the stiffness and solemnity out of musical activities, well and good. Music can be fun, and games and music do share certain common characteristics – teamwork, sense of style, and so on. Games have rules and a well-defined framework which must be understood by player and spectator alike, in the same way that music operates within established criteria – tonality is one such set of 'rules'. A goal or try has a kind of 'meaning' just as music seems to 'mean' something to those who are following it carefully. Furthermore, certain games may be more exciting or better played than others and in a similar way we can see that musical performances tend to be evaluated by the 'spectators'. The play definition of music is certainly on much firmer ground than the hedonistic notion of music as sensuous pleasure. It has a certain 'ring' about it.

But there seem to be at least three important differences that mark off music from games. Music is not 'purely and simply' a game people play. Firstly, games always involve *chance* in a fundamental way. In any good game there is doubt about the outcome; indeed, in the best games we never know until the last moment who is going to win. Even the solitary player of Patience is engaged in a chance-impregnated tussle with 'fate' or luck. A predictable game is usually rather dull. Luck, mistakes and open-ended encounters between players where somebody *loses* something are all part of the games ethos. The opposite tends to be the case with music. We would hope that no player comes off worst in a string-quartet and that mistakes and chance hazards will have been minimized. Of course, in improvised music such as jazz or an Indian raga there is a strong element of playfulness and chance. Even so, much music is thought out whereas most games are played out.

Secondly, music steers us away from 'reality' by presenting us with certain illusions, the illusion of movement for example, whereas games more often have to do with the realities of human encounter or the images of human encounter such as pawns or playing-cards. Music is a very abstract activity compared with the flesh and (literally) blood of boxing or rugby.

And finally, whether we like it or not, music does tend to be rather serious at times. Like primitive rituals, which are often far from playful, music appears to be trying to knock some kind of shape and sense into life's experiences; it seems to be trying to tell us something. Everyone knows of artists and musicians who seem to have been driven on to produce some work or other under difficult circumstances by an inner compulsion. For them at least, Spencer's dictum that the arts occupy the 'leisure part of life' is scarcely appropriate; for them it is work, not play, and important work at that. Perhaps we should make a distinction between the kind of 'play' that children take so seriously and which obviously helps in their development, and 'playing about' as a pastime and relaxation. At any rate we are driven ultimately to a distinction between games and aesthetic activities. The roots of games and music may be similar, but the flowers are very different.

Perhaps at this point we should be clear that the word music is being used in a particular way with reference to particular forms of response to it. We are not, for example, particularly interested here in 'muzak', where music is played to improve industrial output by relaxing or stimulating workers in factories. Nor are we interested in the 'wallpaper' music in restaurants that hides the clink of knife and fork and the grinding of teeth. We are concerned here with the kind of experience we have when we *attend* to music *as though it were saying something to us*. In other words, we are interested in music as a source of *meaning*. We are also interested in the relationship music has with what we call our *emotions*, and we ought to attempt to deal with these two words and the assumptions behind them. Let us take 'meaning' first.

Does music really *mean* anything at all? That is to say, when we listen to music, say at a concert, are we receiving some kind of information and will the person sitting next to us be receiving the same information. Of course, no two people are likely to pick up exactly the same details or to lay stress on the same parts of any incoming information. Even at a lecture or a film, people will notice different things and give different interpretations of what they have noticed. But even so, if all parties are alert and attentive and of reasonably sound mind there will be a consensus of opinion as to what the lecture or film was about. Is this so with music? Stravinsky and Hindemith, to name only two influential musicians, thought not. The latter has said that music is not able to 'express the composer's feelings', and the former thought that music is 'powerless to express anything at all'. (The word 'express' in this context is taken to mean 'communicate'.) Now if we are prepared to say that music expresses nothing, or in other words carries no meaning, we shall find it very hard to justify the time, trouble and money that we might want to see poured into music education. On what grounds can we argue a place in the curriculum for an activity which is not only demonstrably *useless* but also *meaningless?* Also, if a particular piece cannot be said to communicate something to us then composing itself becomes a meaningless activity. As it is, we tend to think that Stravinsky has something to say in his music that is worth hearing, however difficult it may be to describe that 'something'.

We might notice two lines of approach which try to uphold the idea that music *is* able to communicate something to us, that it *does* mean something. The first of these might be called the 'programme' approach. Apart from 'programme-music', which still is very much in evidence in schools, many people seem to think that behind every piece of music is a particular event or mood which the composer is describing. There may be no special story or characters as in *Till Eulenspiegel*, but we might look for autobiographical details of the composer's love-life, state of health or financial position to give us pointers to the music's meaning. Concert programmes sometimes contain statements like 'In the year . . . the composer was in grave financial difficulties and suffering more and more from ill health, which may account for the deep sadness of the *Adagio*'; after which one tends to hear every flat-side modulation as another twinge of pain and every dissonance as yet another bill pushed through the letterbox. Can this really be what the music means? Even the most noble of programmes, whether autobiographical or literary, will tend to destroy or limit our response to the music if we are not careful, as E.M. Forster describes.

I will try to analyse a mishap that has recently overtaken the Coriolanus for Overture. I used to listen to the Coriolanus for "itself", conscious when it passed of something important and agitating, but not defining further. Now I learn that Wagner, endorsed by Sir Donald Tovey, has provided it with a Programme: the opening bars indicate the hero's decision to destroy the Volscii, then a sweet tune for female influence, then the dotted-quaver-restlessness of indecision. This seems indisputable, and there is no doubt that this was, or was almost, Beethoven's intention. All the same, I have lost my Coriolanus. Its largeness and freedom have gone. The exquisite sounds have been hardened like a road that has been tarred for traffic. One has to go somewhere down them, and to pass through the same domestic crisis to the same military impasse, each time the overture is played.[4]

If this is the kind of meaning that Stravinsky wants to root out of music then we may feel very sympathetic. If music does mean anything at all it is not in the form of a second-hand account of a series of incidents better told in words, or perhaps even better still, forgotten altogether. We can be so busy waiting to hear programme effects, the apples being kicked all over the market-place or whatever, that we are unable to notice what is really happening inside the musical utterance.

Apart from this kind of objection, there is so much music that has no obvious programme of any kind which does seem nevertheless to communicate something to us, that we are obliged to consign the whole programme idea to a rather small supporting role in musical experience. Even music with words, opera, oratorio and *lieder*, seem to carry a quite different 'meaning' from the words by themselves. That is why we resist the temptation to tell the singer in *Winterreise* to 'snap out of it', in spite of the fact that the bald sense of the text seems a bit silly, and why agnostics and atheists can be found who enjoy the

St Matthew Passion or *The Dream of Gerontius*. Music is more than a mere reflection of verbal statements.

A second line of approach to musical 'meaning' is more detailed and subtle. It involves a study of what composers actually do; how they use harmonic devices, particular melodic figures or minor intervals, and so on. Albert Schweitzer did it for Bach, pointing out 'weeping' motifs for example. Deryck Cooke, in *The Language of Music*, goes further and attributes particular emotional states to the use of certain intervals, with examples from a wide span of Western music (1959).[5] But no matter how far the detailed analysis may go, with no matter how many examples, when it comes down to locating 'meaning', both writers are driven back once again to words – the words of chorales or the texts of madrigals – to substantiate their theories. We are asked to notice how 'sad' words are set in the minor mode, or how a particular organ figure illuminates the text of a hymn and to extend from this into non-verbal music. Valuable as such work may be, it begs a number of questions. What about other figures in the texture of Choral Preludes which are derived directly from the Chorale itself? What about those parts of *Winterreise* which seem to communicate 'sadness' but happen to be in the major key? But above all, what does the music offer to our experience over and above the meaning of the words? Why bother to add music to something which is perfectly 'meaningful' anyway? Fundamentally, the difficulties of such an approach are similar to those of the 'programme'. Music seems to possess a remarkable ability to speak for itself. Our problem is to try to understand how this happens.

Let us try to break out of these difficult situations and approach the whole problem of 'meaning' in music from a quite different angle. If we think for a moment about meaning in ordinary language we shall realize that there is always something beyond the word or phrase, a concept to which the language refers. Sometimes the referent is easily demonstrated, 'bicycle', for example: at other times it is more difficult to produce the thing to which we refer, 'economic growth', or 'salvation', or even 'sin', though the last of these might be fairly easy to demonstrate. Now let us imagine that instead of trying to find out what a musical phrase meant, we simply wanted to discover whether the word 'pig' had any meaning for a group of people. We might know that the word refers to a grunting, shuffling animal that often ends up in a frying-pan. We could take along a pig and ask what it was, or we could ask for a description of a pig and see if it was accurate. But if we ourselves were not sure what 'pig' meant, and this is the position we are in with regard to music, there would seem to be only one way of finding out whether or not it was a meaningful word. We could ask each member of the group individually to describe a 'pig' and see if the descriptions tallied. If they all said something quite different, that it was a cooking implement, or a kind of bird, or a garment, we could assume that the word was meaningless. On the other hand, if they all agreed at least to the extent that they said it was an animal then we might assume that, more or less, the word was meaningful.

Now this is just the position we are in with regard to music. In the case of a small musical element, say a short phrase, we are not able to produce the referent, the thing that it stands for, nor can we easily say that any individual is giving us the 'right' kind of answer to the question 'What does it mean?' since we ourselves are not at all sure of the answer. We are therefore left with the technique of asking a number of people independently to describe the concept it brings to mind so that we can compare the various descriptions. A consensus of opinion would indicate that the phrase had 'meaning', whereas a rag-bag of different responses would throw doubt on this.

The writer set out on the trail of the mysterious musical referent some years ago. There seemed to be three important considerations. Firstly, it seemed dangerous to use large chunks of music, like a movement of a symphony or even a whole tune, because if such things mean anything at all they may mean a great deal, at any rate too much for clear description. Secondly, it would not have been very helpful to produce sub-musical bits of material. This would be more like asking about the meaning of separate letters of the alphabet than of a word. There remained the questions of establishing a musical style, in other words, of making clear the 'language' or dialect in which the musical statements were made. In music, and perhaps to a lesser extent in ordinary language, the context is vital. (Compare the difference in significance of a cymbal clash in Tchaikovsky's *Romeo and Juliet Overture* and Stockhausen's *Grüppen*.)

Ultimately, simple tonal elements were devised which had two parts to them; a preliminary, style-establishing 'norm', which I call the Basic Unit and a single deviation, which I call the Event. In any presentation of these bits of music to groups of children or adults, the same Basic Unit was always played before a series of different Events. An Event could be a change in pitch, in speed or in instrumental colour, and each set of Events was recorded on tape, most often using piano sound. Here is one such Event preceded by its Basic Unit.

There remained the problem of getting descriptions in a way that they could be compared and analysed. Several previous 'referent-hunters' had made the mistake of assuming that music could best be described in terms of the emotions it made people 'feel'. This is a far more complex situation than at first it may appear, and, not surprisingly, responses were unusually very confused and somewhat vague. In this particular case, the subjects were asked what the music was 'like' just before the end, thus avoiding any suggestion at this stage that how it *felt* was what it *meant*. There were also two extremes to be avoided. One was to allow people to answer in any terminology they liked, thus making comparisons between them impossible: the other was to force limited choices of answers upon them, not allowing a reasonable degree of freedom in description. Ultimately, a device used by psychologists known as the 'semantic differential' proved to be valuable. Here is an example of one of several versions.

active	:	:	:	:	:	:	passive
large	:	:	:	:	:	:	small
light	:	:	:	:	:	:	heavy
stiff	:	:	:	:	:	:	flexible
outgoing	:	:	:	:	:	:	inward-looking
happy	:	:	:	:	:	:	sad

Between each pair of opposite adjectives lie seven spaces. Putting a cross in the space next to 'active' would indicate that we found the musical object extremely active, whereas the space at the other end would indicate an extreme of passivity. The space right in the middle is 'neutral' and the others are 'more or less'. It is really quite easy to

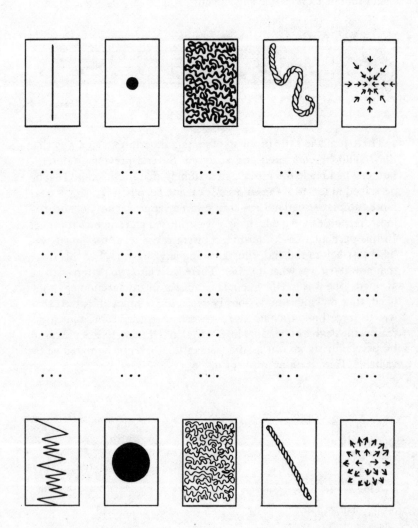

use. The nearer we put a mark to a particular word, the more like that word is our description of what we hear. Thus the music can be described, if we use this particular form, in terms of activity, size, weight, stiffness and so on. These, in fact, proved to be very useful tools of description out of several pairs of adjectives. For every musical Event to be described a separate form was used. Imagine what it would be like to describe a pig and a sparrow using this form. I would guess that it would be easy to sort out the forms used for one and the forms used for the other. What is more, it would be very interesting to see just what the less obvious adjectives produced in the way of answers. So it was when musical Events were described.

With children of seven to nine an alternative version of the form was used which avoided the verbal problems. An artist devised little drawings to be equivalent to the first five pairs of words above and produced what I would call a 'diagrammatic differential'. It looked, finally, like the figure on page 18, and the results it produced were remarkably similar to those given in response to the semantic differential.

Some details of this method of collecting information about musical 'meaning' have been given to show how it is possible to approach the situation via experiment rather than argument. It would be out of place here to enter into a description of the statistical processes employed to aid analysis of these experiments, which were carried out with over 300 subjects ranging from seven-year-old children to music-graduates. One result of it all was that we can now say without fear of contradiction that music is able to communicate specific qualities, that we are able to locate the presence of a referent, that music can be 'meaningful' even at the age of seven and increasingly so thereafter. The answer to the question, 'Has music any meaning?' is therefore, 'Yes it has when people really attend to it and when they understand the style or "norms" within which it operates' (Swanwick, 1973).[6]

Yet we must beware of oversimplifying the issue and especially of adopting the naive view that music is a kind of communication code between the composer and listeners.

composer → music → listener

This presupposes that the composer has some sort of 'message' clear in his mind which he encodes in music, as one might in Morse Code, and which is picked up at the other end of the process by the listener. On this view we might say that the composer is translating his ideas, feelings or beliefs into musical structures, just as a language translator might handle a piece of prose. There are two obvious misconceptions here. The first is that the composer knows what the 'message' is before he makes the music. He may, of course, have some idea of what kind of work is to be undertaken and of the general mood and mode – for example, a symphony in G minor with a fair amount of tension in the harmonies. But otherwise, as we saw earlier, the sound materials at his disposal will tend to impinge on the work as it proceeds and, as musical elements are shaped out of these materials, they in turn will influence and bear upon each other. The second problem is that the listener can have no real certainty that the 'message' he receives was intended by the composer. We might say that the *work* communicates something to us but not so surely that the *composer* does. Hanslick probably had the right attitude years ago:

> Every musical note having its individual complexion, the prominent characteristics of the composer, such as sentimentality, energy, cheerfulness, etc., may, through the preference given by him to certain keys, rhythms, and modulations, be traced in those general phenomena which music is capable of reproducing. But once they become part and parcel of the composition, they interest us only as musical features – as the character of the composition, not of the composer. (Hanslick, 1854, p.72)[7]

What is more, the listener brings to the experience of listening particular values, beliefs and sensitivities which will affect how he hears the work. It may be true, as the experimental work mentioned above shows, that music has a meaningfulness which can be tested out under certain conditions. But it is also true that a musical experience is much more complex than this single level of meaning. We shall examine this area more closely in the following chapter, but for the moment redraw our diagram to show the interaction between composer and musical object and between listener and music.

This also allows us to make much more sense of the role of the performer. On the over-simple view the performer is merely a kind of relay-station to connect the composer's power supply with the listener's receiving apparatus. But now we can see that the performer too builds up a relationship with work, and in some ways may change its emphasis, its very meaning, as he brings his interpretative powers to it. We might notice at this stage that the labels composer, performer, and listener might easily refer to the same person. The composer, after all, may perform his music either complete or in the making, to himself as listener, in order to gauge the impact it makes.

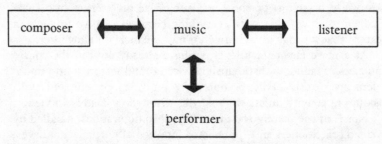

All this may seem somewhat removed from music education, and especially from classroom teaching. But this is really not the case. How we act depends fundamentally on what we believe is true. Let us take the situation where a teacher accepts that music is a kind of message from composers about their feeling, or religious beliefs, or political attitudes. Any scheme of work in music built on this is almost bound to involve an emphasis on the lives of composers, their psychological states, their historical and social background, their relationships with other people and any titles and programmes they may give to their works. We would justify music in any curriculum on the grounds that the messages conveyed by musical objects were of benefit to the moral, social or psychological lives of our pupils. Musical works themselves would tend to have the status of telephone exchanges; places where people are connected together but of no intrinsic value, beauty or significance in themselves. There would seem little point in students making their own works as composers unless they were amplifying some social or emotional message for the good of the community or their own personal and psychological relief.

On the other hand, a teacher who believes that music is merely a pleasurable but meaningless activity is hardly likely to have much professional confidence when it comes to fighting for resources, or negotiating for time with colleagues from other curriculum areas. The appropriate attitude really would be to let things alone. People who wanted to could then choose the musical pleasure they preferred in the same way they might choose between a banana and an ice-cream. It seems hardly worth making a fuss about a syllabus or any scheme of work. We might make a variety of music available to be sampled by pupils, but it is unlikely that we would plan any strategies to develop musical concepts or skills. We should certainly avoid any suggestion that some musical objects are more interesting or powerful than others. After all, one man's meat is another man's poison and who are we to make our personal and subjective preferences into value judgements? On this view everything becomes relative to such an extent that we may as well give up music education altogether.

At a more elementary level we have already noticed the consequences of failing to distinguish between sound materials and music elements. Music easily becomes a sound-management and skill-acquiring activity unless we hold this distinction steadily in view.

Nor is music merely sounds in formal configurations, handled by skilled practitioners and appreciated intellectually. It may not have a simple 'message' but it certainly conveys and brings about meaningful experiences for those who can 'tune in' appropriately. Such meaningfulness resides not in the specific allocation of objects, events or emotions to particular tunes and textures but in the presentation of human *feelingfulness* in symbolic forms (Reimer, 1970).[8] Donald Ferguson (1960)[9] puts it this way: 'music is not a portrayal of chemically compounded emotions. It is a metaphor of experience'.

What this means and how it happens is something of a mystery, though not entirely obscure. Notions of feeling and emotion are frequently brought into play when music and arts education are under scrutiny. It is to these we must now turn.

References
1. LANGER, S. (1942). *Philosophy in a New Key.* Mentor Books: New York, 1951. 175.
2. BRACE, G. (1970). *Music and the Secondary School Timetable.* Exeter University.
3. SPENCER, H. (1911). *Education.* Williams and Norgate.
4. FORSTER, E.M. *Two Cheers for Democracy.* Penguin Books. 135.
5. COOKE, D. (1959). *The Language of Music.* OUP 16ff.
6. SWANWICK, K. (1970). *Musical Cognition and Aesthetic Response. Bull. Brit. Psychol. Soc.* 26, 285-9.
7. HANSLICK, E. (1854). *The Beautiful in Music.* Liberal Arts Press: New York, 1957.
8. REIMER, B. (1970). *A Philosophy of Music Education.* Prentice-Hall: New Jersey.
9. FERGUSON, D. (1960). *Music as Metaphor.* Greenwood Press: USA, 1973 and 1976.

Chapter 2:

The Feelingfulness of Music

If problems of 'meaning' represent one side of our difficulty, then the enigma of 'feeling' or 'emotion' is the other. Most musicians and teachers would agree that music and emotions are somehow related, but to ask *how* they relate opens up a difficult terrain. And yet it is a crucial area for music education, for it is here, in the space between musical objects and human response, that teachers are at work, or should be.

To make matters more difficult, the concept of emotion is very often harnessed to that of 'expression': 'Music expresses emotion' 'We can express emotions through music'. We read that 'some children will express themselves in art, others in writing, others in music', or 'we do not know ourselves until we express ourselves'. Such phrases sound very grand but unfortunately tend to slither around without conceptual support.

Part of the problem is that the word 'express' is used in at least three quite different ways, often confused together. The first meaning attaches to 'express' the idea of discharging, an act of catharsis or purging of feeling, the restoration of emotional balance by release of tension. Thus we might shout in anger, or kick the cat, or have a 'good cry'. These categories of activity are reactions, necessary enough at times but not central to the world of art and music. There is no aesthetic shaping of the action, no structuring and development of the situation. 'What is sometimes called an act of self-expression might better be termed one of self-exposure; it discloses character – or lack of character – to others. In itself, it is only a spewing forth.' (John Dewey, 1958).[1]

The second use of the word 'express' has to do with display of feelings. We signal something about ourselves by the gestures we make, the faces we pull, the actions we perform or by the clothes we wear. In this case we are conscious of the effect we make on others and such self-expression, if carried very far, earns the label 'exhibitionist'.

The third meaning has to do with the making of symbolic forms embodying meaning. We say, 'Am I expressing this clearly?', whether the symbols are linguistic, mathematical or artistic. It seems unfortunate that a blend of the first two meanings tend to overshadow this aspect of expression. As a result we are left with a handful of social and psychological reasons for the arts in education, such as the release of emotions, the development of social confidence, or the finding of the 'self'.

In order to develop a more convincing account of music among the arts and in education we need to hold these ideas of expression in mind and notice one or two aspects of the concept of emotion in music.

The simplest account is similar to the music-as-message idea described in Chapter 1. Composers 'express emotion' in their works and these same emotions are aroused in the listener by the musical apparatus in front of him. There are all kind of problems here. The first one is apparent to anyone aware of the substantial physiological changes that attend emotion experiences. 'An emotion may be defined as a strongly visceralized, affective disturbance, originating within the psychological situation, and revealing itself in bodily changes, in behaviour, and in conscious experience.' (Young, P.T., 1961)[2]

When we take into account the various chemical and glandular changes in the body we can really begin to appreciate the difficulties of the 'expression of the emotions' theory of music. The viscera cannot possibly respond directly in a one-to-one relationship with a long and involved piece of music. The range of emotional states would surely be too great to be fully stirred up in the listener. Also he would feel totally exhausted after the performance and this is not usually the case. People often talk of being stimulated and refreshed by music not always of being drained by a powerful and perhaps harrowing emotional experience.

One of the most extreme statements about emotion and music has been made by Cooke who takes up this point made by Hindemith, that emotions in life cannot follow one another at the speed they would appear in music (op. cit. p.20).[3] Cooke replies: the 'idea that diverse emotions cannot succeed one another swiftly is applicable only to placid temperaments'. (Presumably such temperaments are unable to compose or enjoy music?) Cooke is aware that this will not do, for he postulates *two* levels of emotion, one changeable, the other more permanent and so wriggles out of the problem.

> When we state that a composer, writing a lengthy piece of music over a long period, expresses his emotions in it, we really ought not to have to explain that we mean his deep, permanent, significant emotions, not the superficial fleeting ones called forth by trivial pleasures and disappointments. (Cooke, op. cit., pp.16ff.)

As far as Cooke is concerned, not only are emotions expressed by the composer in his music but they are also felt by the listener in the same way that they were first experienced by the musician. For example, the listener's 'capacity for grief' is aroused by the Funeral March in the *Eroica* symphony. He feels 'as Beethoven felt'. 'Music conveys the naked feeling direct.' Cooke is clearly trying to find a role for emotion in music in the face of provocation by Stravinsky's: 'I consider that music is, by its very nature, powerless to express anything at all, whether a feeling, an attitude of mind, a psychological mood, a phenomenon of nature etc.' (Cooke, p.11.) In trying to locate both emotion and its expression in music, Cooke has put himself in a rather difficult position. Deeply moved by an emotion we may be but is it the real and specific emotion of grief or whatever? Are we really numbed and stunned by sorrow in the *Eroica?* How do we know what the composer felt during the period of time he spent working on this movement? And above all, why should we choose to listen to music that actually makes us feel *grief,* an emotion we would normally avoid?

A modification of the 'expression of emotion' theory is that music expressed an abstract or memory of emotional experience. Music, according to this view, expresses 'joy, sorrow, pain, horror, delight, merriment, peace of mind themselves to a certain extent in the abstract, their essential nature, without accessories, and therefore without their motives.' (Schopenhauer)[4] 'In musical tones the whole scale of our feelings and passions not yet defined in their object, can echo and reverberate.' (Hegel)[5] 'The reactions music evokes are not feelings, but they are the images, memories of feelings.' (Hindemith, 1952).[6] We notice that he is concerned to remove direct, real 'emotion' as such from the situation. Only the 'shadows, dreams, reproductions of actual feelings' are present.

This is a promising refinement though it may seem at first sight even more speculative than the original theory. However, it is supported in an interesting and helpful way by the work of a psychologist, Vernon Lee (1932).[7] Basing her ideas on neurological investigations, she reminds us that any activity, physical or mental, leaves behind in the nervous system a trace of *schema* of itself (Head, 1920).[8] This *schema* will combine with previous remembered experiences to form an ever-developing set of *schemata* which form the basis for recalling the past and planning any future actions. For example, when I get up and walk over to the door I am bringing to the action the *schemata* of many similar experiences, and though I shall not repeat exactly any one of these yet the new pattern or *schema* of movements involved is determined and made possible by them. In other words, all of our experiences leave us with particular patterns of activity in terms of their traces or 'ghosts', which haunt our nervous and muscular systems.

Now if we consider our problems in the light of this we can see that all emotional or feeling states may be characterized by particular patterns of activity – muscular tensions, speeds of action, gait, and so on. For example, depression is often felt and displayed as a set of physical conditions including slow movements, non-emphatic gestures, hesitation and tightness of general posture. Elation, on the other hand, comprises such symptoms as a great deal of unnecessary movement, fast motor speed, emphatic, rhythmical and spontaneous gesture, and self-assertiveness. Anxiety is often revealed in unnecessary movements with perseverance, changeable motor speed, fidgeting, variable forward impulse, and so on. To give a general example, much of the music of Tchaikovsky and Chopin might be described as having about it an 'anxious' quality. How are we able to detect this? Both of them ask for quite a degree of *rubato* in terms of performance tempi (variable forward impulse), and display abrupt changes of speed (ambivalent motor speed), and a certain amount of perseverance (in the form of repeated figures), as well as a trace of 'fidgeting' (to be found in ornamentation and variation). However debatable this might be, I think we might agree that music without a fast motor speec, devoid of unnecessary movement and lacking emphatic and strong rhythmic qualities would not usually be described as 'elated'.

What we are saying then is that the pattern of our actions and sensations, including what we have been calling our emotions, can be presented in music, and what is more, because of the fluid and dynamic nature of music, these patterns are presented 'on the move', just as our feelings are always 'on the move', constantly changing, growing, decaying and merging into one another. Music is in this way a *resemblance* or appearance of feeling: it can show us how feelings *are*. Let us see how this might happen.

In the experiments mentioned above, a number of subjects were asked to describe tiny musical changes in terms that made no specific reference to emotions, except for the happy/sad range. When statistical correlations were made it was discovered that music observed to have about it a degree of 'sadness' also has something of the qualities of passivity, stiffness, heaviness and inward-lookingness. The reverse is true of music that has a degree of 'happiness'. Now this is very close to the way in which we often talk about our emotional states. We say people are 'heavy' with grief, or 'weighed down' with care, or 'light-hearted'. We talk of being 'stiff with worry or fear', and 'free as air'. In other terms then, we might look upon these sorts of sensations as being some of the component parts of particular emotions. Emotions in music are identified by their *schemata*, by their patterns and form, by their dynamic components. I hear music that drags slowly along, that employs the relatively 'heavier' sounds of the lower instrumental ranges, that contains the biting sourness of discords, the rigid gait of dotted rhythms and a constricted tonal and pitch range: therefore I hear a presentation of the abstraction 'grief'; the ghosts (*schemata*) of many griefs are turned abroad to haunt us, embodied in musical tones and durations.

I would suggest that all attempts to clothe these *schemata*, these ghosts, with the flesh and blood of specific experiences will tend to rob the music of its power to move us. Once our minds are involved with recalling an actuality, whether in our own life, or that of the composer, or that of an imposed programme, such as the one described by Forster, they will be unable to continue to attend properly to the on-goingness of the music. Indeed, it is the fusing together of many layers of experience that is part of the power that music has to 'move' us. It is as though feelings and emotions we know are mingled with feelings we may not have experienced, all thrown into the melting-pot, to be moulded into an object of significance, power, or beauty. The result for us is a new and distinctive feeling quality, what has some-times been called the 'aesthetic emotion'. Those who are able to respond to music in this way will often speak of an experience that is transcendental. For there can be no doubt that under certain conditions an aesthetic experience can be a powerful and deep emotional activity, something which takes hold of us and affects the very core of our being.

By now it will have become clear that we have been using the word emotion in three quite different ways.

1. *Emotion* as an intense physiological and psychological experience arising out of particular circumstances and culminating in some kind of action to deal with our inner experiences.

2. *Emotions* as they are presented or re-presented as part of the warp and woof of music. We can recognize them because of their particular mixture of postural components, their gait, pressure and size, their associated *gestures*. All this is within the relative context of the musical style and work

3. *Emotion* that is experienced by the listener as a result of an aesthetic encounter. This kind of experience may be similar in some ways to the first definition of 'emotion' in that there does seem to be a cause – namely the aesthetic object. A tiger is a fearful object, therefore we experience fear: a piece of music is an aesthetic object, therefore we experience an aesthetic emotion. However, we should remember the differences, particularly in that this emotion does not usually find an outlet in action and that an aesthetic object is made for the response it produces and not for any utilitarian reason. (I am aware though that music, like pots, can sometimes be both useful *and* aesthetic.)

Emotions in 'life', emotions as they may be identified in music, and any emotion we might experience as a result of engaging with music are not the same, though we can see how confusions may arise.

Let us return to Cooke and the *Eroica* Funeral March. We might think in the following way: I recognize in the music the heavy, dull stiffness of grief; I experience a strong emotion; therefore I experience the emotion of actual grief. This of course just does not follow and is a muddling of the three uses of the word emotion. Of course we may well experience sympathetically something of the way in which grief 'feels', but the joy we experience from such music goes beyond being merely manipulated to take up, like puppets, attitudes of definite emotional states. A composer is not one of Huxley's 'emotional engineers' *(Brave New World)* who lays on for us a set of experiences at the 'feelies'. On the contrary, we do not just feel specific moods or emotions. What we are offered is not this or that 'life' emotion, but a new and strongly unified experience in which we delight. Such an experience is certainly feelingful but is also meaningful.

And so we are really back to the problem of 'meaning' once again. In the light of these considerations we ought now to recognize two levels of meaning. The first of these is the one already mentioned; it is what the music means *to us,* whether or not it makes sense, whether or not we are able to recognize in it certain sequences of gesture. The second level of meaning really centres on what the music means *for us;* how it uplifts and excites us. The first level is an essential preliminary to the second, it is a matter of *recognition;* in terms of ordinary language it is to be in the position of understanding what is being said. The second level is a question of *relationship,* that of the listener to the work. We may understand what a person is saying and be totally unmoved or uninfluenced by it, we may not be able to relate to it. Just so with music. When we are moved by music let us remember that it is our emotions and not the composer's which are on the move. His mind may have reached out to us in the act of composition but the response is our contribution.

To get this point clear let us consider an analogy given by Professor Reid, who lays great emphasis on this response of individuals to art and music (1969).[9] He is particularly concerned with the aspect of direct relationship with art objects which he calls 'embodied meaning'. We are to imagine we see a man throwing things about. Reid says that we are not particularly concerned with what his actions mean; we just 'see him as angry'. But that there is some meaning in his behaviour is surely not questionable. After all, it is possible to mistake the meaning: he might be throwing things because he is overjoyed by good news or because he is testing the strength of the furniture. We 'read' the signals of his actions along with his facial expression and anything he says. This is what his behaviour means *to us.* What it means *for us* is quite a different matter. We may correctly recognize the gestures as those of anger but may 'see him' as pathetic, mistaken, funny or frightening, depending on our relationship with him, for example, as his wife, a drunken friend, the cause of his anger or a casual passer-by. Reid is quite right when he insists that the direct relationship is central to aesthetic experience, but we must not ignore the importance of the preliminary recognition. In music the appropriate play of such variables as (analogously) weight, stiffness, size, activity and manner of movement has to be grasped before any *appropriate* personal response can take place. For example, a listener who came to the conclusion that the last movement of Beethoven's Fifth Symphony 'expressed' (communicated) a sense of dragging gloom might reasonably be regarded as mistaken. If one were completely bored with the work this could conceivably be our *reaction,* but it could hardly be called an appropriate description of the gestures of the work.

It is on the first level of meaning – meaning *to us* that we may be able to work as teachers. Our influence on the second level is bound to be minimal. So much depends on the individual and his state of feeling at the time.

We can now see that meaning and emotion are intricately related in musical experiences. But the word emotion, though used frequently, is often inappropriate. Fear, anger, love and hate – these seem to be emotions proper with obvious physical symptoms. But what about compassion and nostalgia? Are these emotions? More difficult still, how do we classify contentment or boredom, or the subtle sensations that we experience and which keep us aware of our human existance, providing us with a self-image? How do we regard the sense of intellectual activity which (now and then), we may feel, and how do we rate the basic 'feeling' of consciousness? It is obvious that a lot of 'life' and musical experience is not on the level of the grand emotions. There is comedy as well as tragedy, subtle awareness as well as tremendous impact upon us.

It is much better to settle for the idea of *feelingfulness,* or what Langer calls 'sentience', or consciousness. The high emotions are but one part of this, our life of feeling. Thinking is but another part and may justifiably be seen, not as an antithesis of feeling, but a cross-section of it. After all, we sometimes say 'I feel that . . .' instead of 'I think that . . .'. We put ourselves in a false position in music education if we imagine that emotion and thinking are separate and that we are concerned with the former while colleagues in science or maths are responsible for the latter. The situation is:

not –

but –

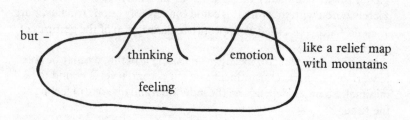

like a relief map
with mountains

Writers on education have tried to wrestle with the problem of educating the emotions, and indeed, musicians have also taken up the idea and frequently attempt to justify music in the curriculum on the grounds that it contributes to 'the education of the emotions'. The phrase is a clumsy one (borrowed from Langer). It is surely *people* who are educated and not their emotions. However, we ought to examine the concept even if it means staying with 'emotion' a little longer.

A great deal of the debate seems to centre on a dichotomy between reason and emotion that goes back at least to Plato and his analogy of the chariot rider, the rational part of man, struggling to control the black horses of emotion. A more recent version of this view has been given by R.S. Peters when he uses the term 'passivity' to indicate that emotions are events that happen to us and with which we have to cope, rather than activities which we ourselves initiate (Peters, 1968).[10] (Thus in a situation of fear our knees 'knock', we do not 'knock' them.) Here we have a concept of emotions as independent forces which need either to be kept in check by reason and social training or (after Spinoza) be overcome by another emotion. They may also be discharged. in cathartic activities like games and the arts. A somewhat different view of the reason-emotion relationship, put forward by G.H. Bantock, is that the emotional aspect of human experience is central and crucial and that in comparison the rational activities are pedestrian and fitful and play a very small role in the life of most people (Bantock, 1967).[11] On this view we should look to educational processes for 'refinement' and development of our emotions, rather than for repression alternating with catharsis. The arts, myths, ritual and religion might then be seen as contributing to an education of the emotions in that they provide symbolic experiences which may both reflect and shape our emotional responses to the world of objects and other people.

Now it is clear from a closer examination of the writing of both Peters and Bantock that concepts of reason and emotion cannot be held apart for long in any consideration of education and the emotions. The affective and the cognitive interact, and it is worth examining these views in a little more detail to bring out the kind of relationships that are envisaged.

For Peters education of the emotions should assist us to develop 'appropriate appraisals', that is to say we should hold well-informed beliefs about the situations in which emotional responses are forthcoming. For example, it would be inappropriate for a husband to be jealous if such an emotion were the result of his misunderstanding his wife's actions. On this view drama and literature may be ways in which our 'capacity for making appraisals' can be extended by an observation of human situations displayed in a play or poetry or a novel and by, as it were, learning lessons from them. Thus our emotions might be said to be educated, in that they are informed by cognitive processes and are only invoked in appropriate situations.

What seems obvious about this way of 'educating the emotions' is that no such education is taking place. No modification of any emotional condition occurs; we merely prevent ourselves from having the wrong emotional reaction to a given situation. This is doubtless very important for a person's education in terms of developing powers of observation, discrimination and judgement, but it does nothing for an emotion when it is considered appropriate. For example, it was once considered by many that it was appropriate to fear, hate and consequently to torture witches. Since we no longer believe in witches in the same way we no longer have these strong emotions in reaction to people who might once have been thought of as witches. But large numbers of people do seem to have strong beliefs about, say, Jews, sexual deviants and communists, and this century has seen plenty of fear, hatred and torture of those who are seen in these categories. Our appraisals have moved on, perhaps been rendered more appropriate, but the emotional responses seem more or less the same as they were. Now it is possible, I suppose, to argue that we might eventually develop a set of appraisals which made no group of people, ethnic or political, or any individual, the object of such emotions. Even so we cannot be said to be educating the emotions as such but will be simply removing the situations which trigger them off and perhaps, eventually, will get rid of them altogether. Indeed the general effect of Peter's statements on the subject is that emotions are to be avoided if possible and if not, then must be endured as an unfortunate experience.

Bantock, on the other hand, suggests a rather different relationship between cognitive and affective elements: 'Human development proceeds, in part at least, out of an ability to make finer and finer distinctions.' An emotion becomes more 'precise' when it is presented in a symbol-structure such as an art product, and many subtle shades of feeling may be displayed which help us towards a process of differentiation, which may refine and structure our ways of responding emotionally to situations. Affect is 'communicable' and it might be possible actually to teach ways of feeling; and Bantock suggests that mothers do this for their children when they give patterns of response to, say, being hurt, disappointed or rewarded. Thus a mother who panics easily, or who worries, or who is perpetually cheerful, may have children who adopt a similar affective stance. (What evidence there is for this is not mentioned.) On this view refinement and communication of emotions are educational objectives rather than correct appraisal and catharsis.

There seem to be two crucial points of difference in the assumptions that underlie these two positions. Firstly, Peters seems concerned only with the extremes of the affective spectrum, with emotions as a rather violent assault on our precarious rationality, states of visceral disturbance such as those manifest in fear, anger, love and so on. Bantock, by his use of the term 'affect', would seem to widen the discussion to include a wide range of feeling experiences which we would not normally identify as 'emotions'. Perhaps amongst these we could list such states as boredom, fatigue, cheerfulness and varying degrees of human affection for people, animals and objects. Of course we would agree that paralysis by fear is an undesirable assault on our 'passivity', but what are we to make of a philosopher's desire to get things clear? Is that affective state to be appraised away or discharged in a cathartic activity? Presumably not, and once we reach the position of recognizing that certain affective states actually need encouragement and development, then Peter's position seems less attractive than Bantock's.

The second point of difference underlying these views is involved with the degree of emphasis on 'symbolic forms' of a non-verbal kind; and here we come to music, which Peters seems to relegate to the role

of catharsis or 'discharge of passivity'. Although he can see that literature and poetry may develop an awareness of the world, the other
arts, 'like music, may be creating, as it were, another world to be aware
of. The latter would therefore be more like games than science or
history' (Peters, 1966).[12] He finds it difficult to accept that the non-
verbal arts have what he calls a 'cognitive content', that they might
carry a meaning which would modify the way in which we view the
world or provide a perspective on life outside of the particular art
experience. Bantock's position here is much closer to Suzanne
Langer's, in that he accepts that affective states can somehow be
presented and communicated through symbolic forms, even those
that do not operate in a verbal medium.

This is really important, especially with regard to music in
education. We have already seen how this symbolic presentation
might come about in music (Chapter 1). Feelings are certainly
able to be expressed in musical objects. We are left with trying to
understand how 'feelings' in music relate to feelings in general and
what benefits, if any, could be said to arise out of musical activities. In
attempting this we shall draw on various aspects of the discussion so
far, but in the first instance consider one further explanation as to how
music is able to produce feelings in those who give it their attention.

This particular view is *relativist* in emphasis, in that it concentrates
on the form and content of music within particular stylistic frame-
works. Meaning and feeling are here very closely related. The most
developed version of this theory is to be found in Meyer (1956):
'Emotion or affect is aroused when a tendency to respond is arrested or
inhibited'.[13] When some kind of action or drive is impeded, we
become aware of an emotion. Meyer's interesting work shows how in
various musical cultures expectancies are produced which are either
fulfilled, delayed, or inhibited. Incomplete figures set up a desire for
completion, to pass over without sounding a note in an accepted scale
series creates a desire to hear that note, and so on. Meyer develops a
theory of music that places importance on *learned* norms and
deviations. A style is established by the composer(s) and learned by
the listener who begins to expect certain things to happen. These
expectations are inhibited to some extent by deviations and surprises.
In course of time certain deviants may become norms and the style is
said to have changed. Western harmony gives clear examples of this,
the chord of the dominant seventh, for instance, is heard as a somewhat violent discord in the sixteenth century and as a comparatively

stable chord by the time of Beethoven. The relativist position has also been clearly put by Hans Keller.

'The background of a composition is both the sum total of the expectations a composer raises in the course of a piece without fulfilling them, and the sum total of those unborn fulfilments. The foreground is, simply, what he does instead – what is actually in the score.' (Keller, 1970).[14] There must be an understood, *learned* background in the light of which musical events take place. Meyer would not go so far as to say that everything is relative and culturally based; for example, the intervals of octave, fourth and fifth seem common to all musical cultures, but *learning* is an essential factor in response to music.

This is a powerful view for those in music education, for by emphasizing *learning* it implies that *teaching* is possible, that we may be helped towards a real understanding of music. This is a much more positive platform than seeing music as catharsis, self-expression or sensuous pleasure. The problem is that it fails to connect musical experience with other experience in any direct way. Music has once again been removed from life, turned into a kind of game, if of an intellectual kind. It seems more likely that expectation and surprise are part of the *mechanism of engagement* with the work. It is how we are kept interested and involved, is how we are brought into action with prediction, speculation and ideas about what is happening and what is likely to happen, and in all this there is obviously likely to be a trace of excitement. But it is *not* the prime source of high aesthetic pleasure. The peak of aesthetic experience is scaled only when a work relates strongly to the structures of our own individual experience, when it calls for a new way or organizing the *schemata,* or traces, of previous life events. This experience of seeing things by a new light is called by Koestler 'bisociation' (1949).[15] It is a 'eureka' experience, what Langer calls the triumph of insight: we discover in the work a 'point of view' that seems to us at the moment to be a kind of revelation. In this area is located what Clive Bell called the 'aesthetic emotion', what Edmund Gurney calls 'emotional excitement of a very intense kind', and what Reid calls a new and individual 'feeling-experience'.

Something of the way in which this experience may be brought about is indicated by McLaughlin (1970).[16] He sees music as made up of patterns of 'tension and resolution' and also that these patterns 'correspond to those of activities in the brain caused by mental and bodily events'. (This view corresponds with that of Vernon Lee's *schemata.*) Now the same patterns may be shared by several groups of activity, mental and physical. That is to say, different activities and experiences may involve somewhat similar sequences of electrical-neural behaviour. A presentation of such a pattern via the tensions of music would, on this theory, give rise to an experience of fusion of a number of past events. It is perhaps better to quote McLaughlin directly at this point, however speculative it may seem.

> For now, at least, we can see that certain patterns have the effect of calling up recollections of many similar patterns from past experiences and that these recollections arise from many different levels of personality . . . and we find ourselves experiencing a synthesis or fusing of many events, many memories, many of the paradigms of existence. This is in itself a new experience, and one which is very much more profound and stirring than the individual experiences of which it is composed. (p.108)

William Empson puts the point in another way (1961).[17]

> . . . whenever a receiver of poetry is seriously moved by an apparently simple line, what are koving in him are the traces of a great part of his past experience and of the structure of his past judgements.

This re-alignment and fusion of various remembered experiences, the play of *schemata*, would seem to be at the root of the most powerfully felt aesthetic experience. It is an experience made from traces of past events, the old seen in new ways. The central point is that the experience is *new*, although it is compounded of elements of each individual's past life. It is its newness and revelatory nature that generates the high excitement that characterizes the encounter of the individual with the art object. Further than this it seems impossible to go at present.

We might then summarize the theory of music that has evolved so far.

1. Music draws on the patterns, *schemata*, or traces of felt-experience by means of precise yet plastic gestures of relative weight, space, movement and tension. In this way and on this level it has 'meaning' or significance and can thus be seen as a vehicle for the communication of 'information'.

2. The framework of operation differs from spoken language in that, unlike dictionary definitions, the 'norms' in music are established and re-established in every piece and period style.

3. The level of predictability varies and fluctuates continually in music experience, thus promoting an active kind of relationship with the

work. We are continually reminded that music is not just a vehicle for our fantasy life. The work is seen to have a 'life' of its own.

4. The highest peak of aesthetic experience is an excitement caused by fundamental re-alignment of the *schemata* we hold to represent past experience. In this way a musical object may be said to have 'meaning' for the individual on a different level of significance from the presentation of feeling gestures in the work.

We ought to be clear that the 'individual' concerned in all four of the above statements may be composer, listener or performer.

It remains to relate this theory of music directly to music education. We ought now to be very clear that any division of the arts and sciences into 'emotional' and 'rational' areas is based on a misunderstanding of the situation. Science is not without its 'eureka' experiences and music is not without cognitive demands. We might notice *four* such cognitive elements in the musical situation, even without reference to composing or performing. Firstly, there has to be on the part of the listener a recognition of the presented 'gestures' that help to form the fabric of a work. This is fundamentally a cognitive as well as an affective process. Secondly, the listener has to build up norm concepts as a general frame of reference in which he locates such 'meaning' as is presented in the work. Thirdly, he has to be able to predict a future during the work as it progresses in order to formulate expectations which may or may not be met in the course of the music. Fourthly, the listener may undergo a change of *cognitive perspective* as a result of the particular encounter with the work and its relationship to his past experience of both music and living.

To be helped towards a perspective on the life of feeling is surely an *educative process.* We are helped to structure and understand certain modes of feeling by the mapping out, charting and abstracting of affect in music and the arts. Emotions in music are not so much 'discharged' or 'disciplined' (in the sense of being trained to behave themselves) but are presented for us to *understand,* to clarify what before might have been undifferentiated and confused. As Bantock says: 'Human development proceeds, in part at least, out of an ability to make finer and finer distinctions'. It also proceeds out of an ability to re-order, to restructure experience, to make one concept out of many random experiences. This task of formulation and refinement is in the hands of the makers of art-works. The arts resound with ideas about human feeling and (Koestler's term), 'bisociate' instinct and intellect. Small wonder that involvement with the arts frequently induces a distinctive excitement, sometimes called the 'aesthetic emotion'. Hanslick is aware of it, Reid and Edmund Gurney acknowledge it: we either experience it or not. Vernon Lee's subjects gave strong accounts of the experience. It is the ultimate pleasure in the aesthetic situation, though we might notice certain less heady pleasures that rarely rise to the level of being graced with the name 'emotion', admiration of technique, pleasure in seeing the point of a work, delight in the clarity or some other quality of the presentation, and so on.

We have seen that music has a precise public meaning on one level and a profound meaning for the individual on another level, and it has been argued that it straddles the affective and cognitive areas of experience by identifying, clarifying and structuring feeling. Music is one mode of understanding the world and our experience of it, it is a *way of knowing the affective* and knowing *through* feeling.

> Life holds its shape in the modes of dance and music
> The hands of craftsmen trace its patternings. (James McAuley)

From this basis, however provisional, we can move forward more confidently to a consideration of the ways in which people might come to know music, to the parameters of music education.

References
1. DEWEY, JOHN (1934). *Art as Experience*. Capricorn Books: 1958. 61-2.
2. YOUNG, P.T. (1961). *Motivation and Emotion*. New York. 597.
3. COOKE, D. (1959). *The Language of Music*. OUP.
4. SCHOPENHAUER. *The World as Will and Idea*.
5. HEGEL. *Aesthetics*.
6. HINDEMITH (1952). *The Composer's World*. Harvard. 38ff.
7. LEE, VERNON (1932). *Music and its Lovers*. Unwin. 44ff.
8. HEAD, H. (1920). *Studies in Neuralogy*. Oxford. 605-606.
9. REID, L.A. (1969). *Meaning in the Arts*. London. 71.
10. PETERS, R.S. (1968). *The Logola Symposium on Feeling and Emotions*.
11. BANTOCK, G.H. (1967). *Education, Culture and the Emotions*. Faber. 65-86.
12. PETERS, R.S. (1966). *Ethics and Education*. Allen and Unwin.
13. MEYER, L.B. (1965). *Emotion and Meaning in Music*. Chicago.
14. KELLER, HANS (1970). *Towards a Theory of Music* in the *Listener*, 11 June 1970.
15. KOESTLER, A. (1949). *Insight and Outlook*. Macmillan: London.
    and (1964). *The Act of Creation*. Pan Books.
16. McLAUGHLIN, T. (1970). *Music and Communication*. Faber.
17. EMPSON, W. (1961). *Seven Types of Ambiguity*. London.

Chapter 3:

The Parameters of Music Education

Music is queer stuff, something like a soap-bubble in a way: when floating about it appears real and substantial but when 'analysed' with a pin or finger-nail we are left with a slightly damp nothingness. Because music is so ephemeral it presents teachers with severe difficulties. It has to be handled and understood as it moves on through time; managed 'on the wing'. It is also very abstract with practically no possibilities for representing obvious 'subjects'. Even the simplest tune bears no palpable relationship to any single equivalent object or event outside itself.

Music shares its problems of being a time-dependent art, though not its difficulties of abstraction, with drama and the theatre. Theatrical events resemble music in many ways; in ensemble playing, in bringing a work 'off' in time, in the risks of performance, in relating the imagination of actors and director to the intentions of the author, and in the need to win the attention of and *rapport* with audiences. But the resemblance ceases when it comes to trying to talk to one another about a particular working situation. An actor and director may discuss the meaning and intention behind certain lines and gestures. They may discuss character and plot. In doing so they are concerning themselves with the very stuff of the play (or improvisation) and not merely with technicalities. Musicians are more likely to settle for technical discourse: 'watch the dynamics', or 'use less bow', or 'Ligeti defines his *Volumina* as a piece consisting entirely of stationary and variously changing note clusters'.

In other words, it is hard to talk about music without talking about something else – technique, style, historical background – anything but the experience that music seems to present to us and our personal response to it. Yet we acknowledge that these alternatives are by themselves insufficient and that we do have other criteria in mind when we say things like 'he has a good technique but plays so unmusically', or 'her sense of style seems impeccable but there was no sense of performance', or 'it is a very clever composition but it leaves me cold'. Like money in general and 'discipline' in schools, we affirm the existence and value of real musical experience when we cannot get any.

Because this experience is sometimes elusive and because music is manifested in such a variety of settings and takes on many different ways of functioning, it is crucial for those of us concerned with music education to evolve a clear view of our procedures which may be held steady, no matter in what particular situation we may find ourselves. Composing, practising, working with choral and instrumental groups, rehearsing steel-bands, getting into popular music, penetrating the worlds of *avant-garde* composers or Indian improvisors, helping someone to play the clarinet or trombone, dealing with an oboe reed or ring-modulator, reading about historical aspects of opera or the symphony, discussing the music of Messiean – these are all in *some* way to do with music. Can anything of value be said that bears upon all these instances and many more besides? I think it can, and I also believe that some of the confusion in which we find ourselves is caused by a failure to recognize the common ground upon which music and music education rests, whatever forms they may take.

I believe it is especially helpful to map out the various ways in which people actually relate to music, how we connect with it, how we come to *know* it. For a musical object is surely a knowable entity, and we can know it more or less. Obviously there are times when we are vaguely aware of sounds around us, on the radio, in film, on television and in public places – supermarkets and churches. At such times there is often what has been called 'a state of music'. We *know* it is there, that is all, and we give it little of our attention. It is clearly not the job of any teacher to settle for this state of affairs. We are concerned to help people get into music in a more active way and find in the experience of music a more positive response. It is one thing to overhear and quite another to listen to and fully engage with music as though it mattered. Knowing music is something like knowing a *person*. We cannot really believe that we *know* people because they happen to be around us, or because we pass them in the street or stand crushed together on a train or bus. This is no more knowing a person than to have the statistical information that someone weighs so much, is six feet tall, lives in Leeds and owns a car and a washing machine.

We should accept that a teacher's role involves a concern for strengthening the relationship between pupils and music. This involves increasing attention to and the level of involvement with music in a conscious and deliberate way. The media are better equipped than teachers to generate a 'state of music' and they do it very well. The individual teacher is better employed promoting what I call *the integrity of the particular*.

Even to talk about 'music' as we have been doing, as if it were a single and simple thing, is to run the risk of underestimating its potential power and infinite variety.

The power of music and the incredible number of different *musics* spreading out laterally across countries and cultures and historically back in time, place upon teachers an obligation to assist pupils to develop not merely a tolerance of a limited musical idiom but also an ability to approach actively and willingly music from a range of styles and contexts. This flexibility across idioms and cultures is best helped by playing a variety of roles in relation to music. Just as knowing people really well involves us in personal contact across a variety of different meetings, and in relating to them on various levels, so it is with musical relationships. People need multiple opportunities for meeting up with music, homing in from different angles in order to become aware of its richness of possibilities.

It is all too easy to become fixed in position as, say, a flautist or pianist, or a church organist or chorister, or a musicologist or composer or mere 'listener' without the vitalizing experience of coming to know how music feels from alternative positions and within the context of different relationships.

There are then two crucial educational points to be kept in mind as we consider the modes of relationship between people and music. The first of these is that teachers should be concerned with the promotion of specific musical experiences of one kind or another. The second is that students should take up different roles in a variety of musical environments. People will find their individual paths into particular areas of music. It is our responsibility to keep the various roads clear and not insist that there is only one narrow avenue, perhaps the one we took ourselves. The crucial thing is to seek out those activities which give direct involvement and not to skate about on *quasi* musical enterprises.

Direct involvement can be seen under three headings. They are *composition, audition* and *performance;* CAP for short. However, there is often a good deal of confusion here and it would be as well to indicate straight away exactly what is intended.

Composition

Under this heading is included all forms of musical invention, not merely works that are written down in any form of notation. Improvisation is, after all, a form of composition without the burden or the possibilities of notation. Composition is the act of making a musical object by assembling sound materials in an expressive way. There may or may not be experimentation with sounds as such. A composer may know what the materials will sound like from past experience in the idiom. Whatever form it may take, the prime value of composition in music education is not that we may produce more composers, but in the insight that may be gained by relating to music in this particular and very direct manner.

Audition

Why use such a stuffy word? There comes a point where to talk of 'listening' just will not do. Listening is first on the list of priorities for *any* musical activity, not just hearing a record or attending to someone else in performance. Playing a scale evenly, deciding on a particular timbre for a moment in time in a composition, rehearsing and practising a piece, improvising, tuning an instrument; they all involve listening. Audition, however, means attending to the presentation of music as an *audience.* It is a very special form of mind often involving empathy with performers, a sense of musical style relevant to the occasion, a willingness to 'go along with' the music, and ultimately and perhaps all too rarely, an ability to respond and relate intimately to the musical object as an aesthetic entity. It resembles a state of contemplation. I am not thinking only of the somewhat rarified situation of the concert hall. To come across a brass band in the street, a particular record played in a disco or a snatch of tune on the radio, and to focus in on that to the virtual exclusion of all else is to become an *auditor*, an engaged listener. We become absorbed in and changed by the experience. We are thinking here of the crucial *aesthetic* experience. Audition is the central reason for the existence of music and the ultimate and constant goal in music education. We are reminded of Pepys who tells us in his diary of 27 February, 1668 that he went to a performance of wind music:

> which is so sweet that it ravished me and, indeed, in a word, did wrap up my soul so that it made me really sick, just as I have formerly been when in love with my wife . . . and makes me resolve to practice wind music.

The same kind of experience is described by Steinbeck in *The Grapes of Wrath*, when the guitar player entertains the 'dust-bowl' refugees in the camp and 'in the dark the eyes of the people were inward, and their minds played in other times, and their sadness was like rest, like sleep'.

These people were surely *auditors* in the strongest sense of the word.

We might notice that in both of these instances the experience of being an auditor often arouses a desire to become more actively involved. Pepys was resolved 'to practice wind music', and Steinbeck's dispossessed farmers 'each wished he could pick a guitar, because it is a gracious thing'. This brings us to the third group of activities.

Performance

This needs little amplification here, except to notice that performance is a very special state of affairs, a feeling for music as a kind of 'presence'. We sometimes say that a performance 'didn't come off' or that someone appeared to lack a 'sense of performance'. Just as an auditor is focusing in tightly on what he hears, so is the performer but usually on the basis of previous preparation, with the special obligation of creating a future for the music as it evolves, and with a sense of a present audience, no matter how small or informal. There is usually an element of risk, not merely technical but in a very real sense concerned with whether the music will happen or not, whether the special, almost magical quality will emerge or whether, at the other extreme, the whole thing becomes a bore.

Once we accept that composition, audition and performance are activities central to music, we are then obliged to notice that a lot of what takes place under the heading of 'music teaching' seems to be concerned with something else. That 'something else' may include coping with some aspect of traditional notation, or 'aural training'. It may be trying to deal with the technical problems of an instrumentalist, or getting the choir to sing the right notes in some kind of balance and with a good blend of tone. It could be learning how to use a synthesizer, or to generate and extend the range of possible sounds produced through a tape recorder. It might be analyzing a musical work, or getting up information about the composer, the period or the compositional techniques involved. None of these things are central to the experience of music, though sometimes they may help to bring about better composition, audition or performance. Things go wrong in music education when they become ends and not mere means. Technical practice and rehearsal should lead to performance, however informal. Knowledge of music history, style and compositional technique is only useful to musical experience if it informs composers, auditors and performers and strengthens these activities. There is, no doubt, a place for musicological studies of an historical kind undertaken for their own sake, but if so we are involved in the discipline of historical study, not music.

These various activities peripheral to experience of music itself can be grouped under two headings of *skill acquisition* and *literature studies*. Skill acquisition takes in such things as technical control, ensemble playing, the management of sound with electronic and other apparatus, the development of aural perception, sight-reading abilities and fluency with notation. Under literature studies we include not only the contemporary and historical study of the literature *of* music itself through scores and performances but also musical criticism and the literature *on* music, historical and musicological. These then are our five parameters of musical experience – three of them directly relating us to music and two more having supporting and enabling roles; C(L)A(S)P for short.

C(L)A(S)P

C	*Composition*	formulating a musical idea, making a musical object
(L)	*Literature studies*	the literature of and the literature about music
A	*Audition*	responsive listening as (though not necessarily in) an audience
(S)	*Skill acquisition*	aural, instrumental, notational
P	*Performance*	communicating music as a 'presence'.

The main purpose of separating these clusters of activities under the mnemonic of C(L)A(S)P is, strange though it may seem, to put them back together more effectively than is often the case. We note that people who seem to be specializing in a particular area, say in composition or performance, or perhaps in the teaching of particular skills, tend to influence one another. Composers are often stimulated by performers who have special sensitivity and technical (skill) control. On the other hand performers need to reach out for new experiences and stimulation of what composers produce. They are also much influenced by the attitudes of their auditors and by the erudite comments of musicologists and critics. Indeed, research in musicology seems to add new 'old' works to the performing repertory at a rate almost comparable with the composition of twentieth-century pieces. People who are primarily auditors are supposedly influenced by everyone else, though some would say not as quickly and powerfully as they might be. They in turn affect composers and performers by the concert tickets and records they buy and through the applause they give or withhold. There is no need to go on multiplying examples of such cross-influences.

More important though, C(L)A(S)P provides a model for education. It gives a framework for generating potential musical experiences, in the light of the two crucial principles of procedure indicated earlier, that teachers are trying for specific experiences but across a wide range of activities. Here we have the areas from which we draw the specific experiences that teachers must have concern for. At any particular moment we are bound to be active somewhere in C(L)A(S)P or not involved with music experience at all. But as teachers we are also concerned to activate experiences for pupils that cross and recross these five parameters, or at least some of them. They should be related. Skills without performance is an arid affair, performance without skills is surely to be avoided, composition without the stimulation and models of other composers' works experienced in audition is unlikely; the auditor who is not also active in music in some other way is comparatively rare; knowledge of musical literature without a liking for musical audition or even some fluency in music-making seems an irrelevant occupation.

On this point, Ian Lawrence (1977) has drawn out attention to the attitude of a number of composers which reinforces the view being put forward. Hindemith believes that music education should be 'comprehensive', that the teacher should himself perform, compose, analyse and be historically aware.[1] Lawrence cites Quantz (1752) saying 'The student must beware of a master who understands nothing of harmony and who is no more than an instrumentalist', and Wagner stressing the importance of being an auditor: 'A musician's aptitude for his art is best estimated by the impress which other people's music leaves upon him.'

Also we note the comment by C.P.E. Bach: 'Observe how musicians always listen to each other and modify their performance so that an ensemble may reach the desired goal'. Even in the act of performing and rehearsing we need to play the role of auditors, responsive to the aesthetic possibilities of the work.

Although the situation of these composers is very different from that of students, especially children in school, yet it would surely be wrong to assume that there is no resemblance between them. After all, children are not completely different from adults and the psychological act of composing or performing has not fundamentally changed over the years and does not alter radically across an age range.

One value of being clear about C(L)A(S)P then is that it puts (L) and (S) in perspective. It also enables us to specify at any given moment what kind of an activity we are involved with. Additionally, it functions as a kind of valency model. It reminds us to 'only connect'.

I ought to make clear what I am *not* saying. Firstly, there is no suggestion that students should not specialize in some single area of C(L)A(S)P. This is bound to happen almost from the beginning of involvement with music. Secondly, I am not insisting that everyone should necessarily have substantial experience in all five areas, only that wherever possible people ought to be encouraged to be involved with music in as many ways as possible, especially in the early formative years.

Thirdly, it is not being recommended that, for example, all students in colleges and universities should necessarily be required to take separate courses in each area. This happens to a certain extent already and the result is that we tend to get little disconnected units of music history, fragments of 'harmony and composition', some instrumental teaching, choral and orchestral performance on special occasions, and, more rarely, help with audition. The important thing is that *individual teachers* should endeavour to illuminate the particular task in hand with light from other aspects of C(L)A(S)P, whatever their specialism. The reluctance to do this is most clearly seen in our universities and colleges of music and there are underlying difficulties in the present organization of courses and quality of staffing. All the same, it does seem strange when students appear not to regard the pieces they happen to be practising (S) as possible candidates for performance (P), no matter how formal and, in a sense, unfinished. It seems odd that these same works often get no mention in examination papers on music history (L) and that they may not have heard performances of them or similar works (A). It is also slightly regrettable that their 'harmony and composition' exercises often include no attempt to utilize the growing sense of style gained from contact with the particular work in hand as a basis for composition (C) or that work in 'keyboard harmony' manages to avoid improvisations along the lines of the same piece. Obviously there are exceptions and some bright students make their own integrations. The question is, are the others helped at all in this way and is the spread of styles wide enough, bearing in mind the diversity of music today?

In schools the position is sometimes a little better, though we still occasionally get music wrapped up in 'singing' and 'theory' lessons, and never the twain shall meet. More recently we have seen an emphasis on children as 'composers', but this has sometimes meant 'and as nothing else'. Yet the composer in each of us needs the stimulation of the auditor and performer that we are able to be.

Let us consider a few actual cases where music education seems to falter because of a failure to recognize the inevitability of C(L)A(S)P relationships. The first example comes from abroad: it is often easier to see the speck of dust in someone else's eye!

1. An American high school band rehearses most days of the week and gives very polished performances at football games and elsewhere. Yet many of the students appear to get little pleasure as auditors, and rarely explore the activity of composition. Two of the outcomes seem to be that the actual performances, though very slick, seem mechanical and in many cases the instrument is more or less given up when students leave school. (One American student told me that she stopped playing the clarinet after thirteen years of being in a school band. She had never really liked the sound of the instrument!). Is this music education or is it more like a training as an instrumental operative? Why is there such a negative response to music after all that exposure? I would suggest that it is because music had defined itself for these students only as skill acquisition and performance along a limited range of musical styles. Aesthetic response to music through audition is unlikely to occur when

people are kept under so much technical pressure: they are just too busy. When they are responsive it is along too narrow a front.

2. A church choir rehearsal is in progress. 'Accompanied by robust organ sound we are hurled through ten hymns, two psalms, six anthems and part of a cantata. The notes and the words (so many words) are mastered and nothing is likely to fall apart. But one comes away longing for a sensitive phrasing or a few cadences drawn together with a feeling of musical arrival, for a few suspensions felt as tension and release, and above all for a sense of performance in at least one of the items on the rehearsal agenda. The whole time has been spent in skill acquisition. We have not begun to notice the musical intentions of the composers, or take into account how the auditors (congregation) will respond on Sunday.

3. A class in school is attempting to perform a contemporary piece called *Sound Patterns I*, by Bernard Rands. It is difficult. There are complex notational devices to be understood, conductor's signals to be watched and a contemporary style to be mastered. After fifteen minutes they are obviously a little confused and not without signs of boredom. Yet the work looks as though it might have possibilities and the teacher is reasonably effective and relates quite well to the pupils.

Once again a major source of difficulty is that we are in the wrong area of C(L)A(S)P at the wrong time. There are many skills and concepts to be learned before this work can be embarked upon. There has to be a fairly substantial exposure as auditors to works of this kind and some active experience as composers (in groups) working with similar sound materials and techniques. In a second school the same work gets a sensitive performance for just those reasons. The pupils develop appropriate skills (S) and explore the compositional possibilities (C) of similar materials to those used by Rands, which in turn leads to the development of more skill (S). They perform (P) and hear other group compositions and short excerpts from composers working in similar ways (A). They then have a platform from which to reach for *Sound Patterns I* (P). There has, incidentally, been some discussion (brief) about the composers involved and the evolution of the newer techniques and music styles (L). All areas of C(L)A(S)P have been penetrated: experience in one illuminates and reinforces another.

Enough has been said to expose the basically simple but possibly helpful model C(L)A(S)P. It has many well-tried practical possibilities, and some of these will be considered in a subsequent chapter. Fundamentally, C(L)A(S)P is only a theoretical formulation of what happens in countless instances of good music teaching and of what is missing from much bad professional practice in music education. The value of an analysis of this kind is that it draws together in a simple structure what previously may have been disconnected and fragmented. The usefulness of the model for teachers at work is two-fold. In the first instance we can helpfully, at any moment in teaching, ask in which area we are engaged and where the emphasis of the next task might be. If we find ourselves working with a great deal of (L) and (S) but not much C, A and P, we probably ought to review what we are about. On the other hand, to encourage C in the interests of self-expression or some such notion without developing any (S) would also require scrutiny. And again, of what value are activities under any of the parameters unless the central A is being developed? Secondly, we are able to generate teaching strategies by consciously looking for precise and specific connecting links between activities across the five parameters. Starting somewhere we can go anywhere, constrained only by the integrity of the particular activity of the moment. Later on we shall look at examples of this way of working in a variety of settings.

We are now in a position to assemble the main issues raised so far into a structure that may illuminate the total field of music education. Such light, however small, is needed badly. We tend to be blown about by winds of change from many quarters without much idea of navigating the ship of music education and without any sense of direction. Consequently, we are easily taken off course. The right-wing of our profession insist on 'standards', and the 'basics' of music. This usually turns out to mean aural skills, the theory of notation and some knowledge of music history: in other words, lots of (S) and (L). The left-wing will have none of that, but insist on self-expression and 'creativity', (a word in need of attention later) or immersion in the 'music of the pupils', which usually means the history and social background of pop, rock and reggae, this being just another version of (L) often without much (S). Both views have something to offer but fail to centre in on the crucial aesthetic responsiveness which is the fundamental reason for the existence of music and music education. Let us at least try to get the perspective right. To do this we return briefly to the ideas in the earlier chapters and initially to the 'listener'.

Because we have now considered the parameters of music education in terms of *activities* that people do and *roles* that they play, we can no longer tolerate the abstraction of a 'listener'. The act of attentive and responsive listening, with aesthetic understanding as part of the experience, may be simply termed *audition* from now on. The interactive bond between a musical object and the act of audition may then be pictured in the following way.

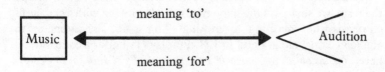

In Chapter 2 we noted that meaning *to us* refers to the discernable qualities or character of the musical objects, its gestures and surface 'meaning'. We saw in Chapter 1 how it is possible to find a kind of referent for music, how musical events can be described in different ways using analogies of relative weight, activity, size and so on. Meaning *for us*, on the other hand, indicates what Reid calls the 'embodied meaning' of personal relationship with the particular work. On the first level of meaning an auditor brings previous experience of *music* to the work; a sense of style, an aural ability to discriminate tunes, textures and timbres, a set of expectations. The work conveys to the auditor its particular gestures and felt qualities, and also its idiosyncrasies, its deviations from the expected norms. When the relationship is right the act of audition is both cognitive and affective, even on the first level of meaning. On the second level (meaning for), the auditor brings his experience of *living* to the work; a sense of vitality, memories or *schemata* of past events, an attitude to human feelingfulness. The work communicates to the auditor a perspective on life as it is felt along with a new sense of fusion, an expansion of possibilities beyond the commonplace. Some readers may find such metaphysical statements difficult to accept. In which case we can simply note that the act of audition and a music object are interactive in a two-way process and that audition takes place on the basis of other life-experiences, which we might call *feeling*.

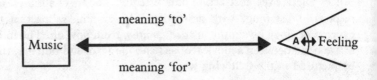

If we turn now to the act of *composition,* in the widest definition of the term, we shall find the same two basic themes but with a change of emphasis from 'meaning' to 'making'. This is not an easy matter to elucidate and I am grateful to J.N. Findlay (1968) for a contribution here: *'for an object to come before us aesthetically it must do so* perspicuously *and* poignantly'.[2] 'Perspicuous' signifies something clear, lucid, intelligible: 'poignant' has to do with an impact upon us which is intense, impressive or stirring. Clarity and intensity then: these concepts are very close to *meaning to* and *meaning for.* The first emphasizes recognition, how the object seems to us; the second is more concerned with our personal response, the impression made by the experience. *Clarity* and *intensity* will serve to indicate the process central to the act of composition, and the ends towards which a composer strives as he fashions his musical objects. They are sometimes linked with form and feeling respectively. As we saw in Chapter 1, the process is always two-way. A composition begins to assume a life of its own very early on, interacting with and modifying any original intentions. Even so, the composer too has a life of his own and something of his felt experience will manifest itself in the work. The act of composition is related to what we have called life-experiences or feeling, in a similar way to the act of audition.

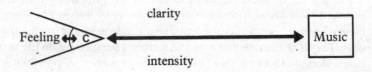

We must bear in mind that we are talking of roles we play and not of professional careers; of activities and not of particular people. Thus the act of composition is possible only when alternated with audition and possibly performance. A composer must surely sample his own work as auditor and try it out as performer.

The act of *performance* can be seen in a similar light. We have already noted that performance involves a sense of presence, the presence of a vital musical object, developing and on the move; and that this differs from a merely accurate rendering, in that it is *alive*. The performer's special role is to mediate directly between the work and its auditors. (Not between composer and auditor!) The sense of presence is amplified by two elements distinctive for performance but closely related to our two levels of 'meaning' and to the concepts of clarity and intensity respectively. These elements are *projection* and *impact*. The work is projected with clarity and sense of meaning in the surface gestures, but is also felt as impact, with intensity of feeling and the personalized meaning of the deeper level. Thus in a strange way the act of performance is a blend of composition and audition simultaneously. It is projected as though being composed (an illusion deliberately cultivated by the memorizing of the score) but felt with impact, as audition, with fresh *meaning to* and *meaning for* each time it is played.

The presentation will be informed not only by a study of the particular gestures in a work within the stylistic context but also by the personal feelings of the performer. Idiosyncratic qualities of thought and temperament are bound to be drawn into any performance and we can often recognize the personal 'stamp' of a player, the distinctive interpretation.

Our model so far then looks like this:

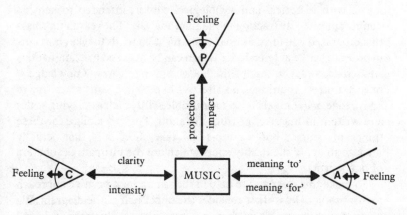

We can now summarize the main argument: musical objects are the focus of musical experience and therefore of music education; this experience is only acquired through the activities of composition, audition and performance; each of these three areas involves a relationship with music that is distinctive in emphasis; audition is prime among them; musical experience refers to, and at its most powerful, reformulates the ways in which we *feel* life.

The most rewarding areas of attention for music educators are the activities of composition, audition and performance *at the first level of meaningfulness,* the search for clarity, meaning 'to' and projection of musical image. The second level, of intensity, meaning 'for' and impact, is a highly personal affair and is psychologically very complex. We are not able to work directly in this area as teachers and it is highly dangerous to believe that we can. Some interesting attempts have been made to cope with this problem, notably by Witkin (1974)[3] and Ross (1978)[4], and we shall consider these in the final chapter.

It is quite helpful at this stage to extend our model to take in skill acquisition and literature studies in order to see the kinds of relationships involved. To avoid confusion, the parameter of performance is omitted, though it could be imagined as standing up at right angles from the central dotted lines.

The central horizontal lines related composition and audition with music (and performance similarly) are the main concern of music education. If we stray far from these direct and living relationships we run the risk of missing the point of music as aesthetic experience. It is all too easy to overlay a comparatively simple and nature response to music with historical and sociological clutter, intended to help no doubt, but often distracting in the final analysis. The reason for this is that organized and formalized music education tends to take short cuts in order to arrive at knowledge which can be assessed in examinations and which is easy to teach from books and in lectures. Knowledge *of* music, a direct cognitive and affective experience, thus gives way to knowledge *about* music or to measurable skills, such as playing scales and writing in manuscript from dictation. There is a place for these things of course, but we must not take short cuts that actually manage to *avoid* the beauty spots which are the ultimate destination of our journeys.

To make this clear and to help in the search for a positive approach to this problem let us first consider the upper half of the diagram. We know that there can be no short cut from musical objects to style and

A Comprehensive Model of Musical Experience

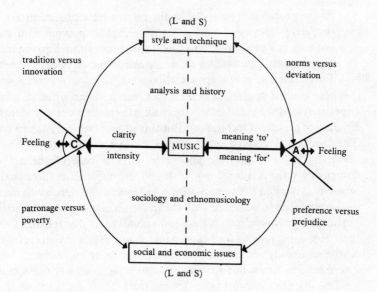

(L and S)

style and technique

tradition versus
innovation

norms versus
deviation

analysis and history

Feeling   C   clarity   MUSIC   meaning 'to'   A   Feeling
                intensity   meaning 'for'

sociology and ethnomusicology

patronage versus
poverty

preference versus
prejudice

social and economic issues

(L and S)

Note: C = Composition
       L = Literature studies
       A = Audition
       S = Skill acquisition
       P (not shown) = Performance

technique (up the dotted line) via analysis and history. These activities only have significance for music and music education when they are related to actual composition, audition and performance. Failure to grasp this point may well account for the strange phenomenon of some music students who appear *not* to like or respond to music in any significant way. Findlay helps to make the point more strongly (1968, op. cit.).

> Some people intensely dislike the intense gaze or gazed stare of aesthetic enjoyment, and go to any lengths to avoid it or discourage it. But to do so is to substitute connoisseurship, historical information, factual analysis, or the manipulation of value-tickets, for genuine aesthetic appreciation.

There can, of course, exist a relationship between direct musical experience and skills and literature studies (here considered under the heading of style and technique). But this cannot be via any short cut. The horizontal and peripheral lines of the model indicate some possibilities for a positive approach. In the case of the act of composition, the relationship to style and technique is felt through the tensions generated between *tradition* and *innovation*. Decisions made in this area should be linked with the quest for clarity and intensity in particular works and involve an individual quality of feeling. Only then does concern with tradition or innovation aspire to the level of an aesthetic activity; otherwise we have pastiche or experiment, both interesting at times but devoid of artistic significance, the former tending to communicate platitudes and the latter failing to communicate through excess of novelty. The river of composition needs to be fed by all three tributaries.

1. awareness of tension between tradition and innovation
2. the clarity of the work in the making
3. the relationship of the work to personal experience (intensity)

Similarly, the act of audition can only be related to problems of style and technique through the perception of *norms* and *deviations*. To be able to project a set of expectations and to experience the interest, the engagement and excitement when these are inhibited or eventually realized is to understand the secrets of the style and manner of the work before us. Otherwise the butterfly lies dead and dismantled on the table, no longer a mobile object of beauty with aesthetic qualities but the subject for scientific inquiry. It is possible that certain forms of analysis of music may be helpful in enhancing our response to it, but if so we must once again sense the interaction of three forces.

1. Perception of norms and deviations
2. meaningfulness of the particular work (meaning 'to')
3. relationship of the work to our experience of living (meaning 'for')

The lower half of the diagram makes a similar point, but this time with reference to the more recently evolved disciplines of sociology and enthnomusicology. Here again, there can be no short-cut to music via these activities from a starting point of social, economic or political issues. For example, a study of musical objects in terms of the way they are generated by different social groups will have no aesthetic significance for those embarked on such a course, nor will it shed any light on fundamental aesthetic processes. The attempted link is factual and discursive in emphasis (literature studies) unless the music under scrutiny becomes meaningful and feelingful through the activities of composition, audition and performance. What we have is still a substitute, interesting perhaps in its own right, but *not* aesthetic education. To take a specific instance, a knowledge of the history and social background of pop music is just as non-aesthetic as the study of any specified period of musical history or particular style. Such a study only becomes aesthetically charged for the auditor when there is an attempt to link social and economic issues to music via awareness of preference and prejudice. This is no longer a merely objective description of social issues but a challenge to discover 'meaning' in unfamiliar music and relate it to our life experience.

In the same way, we might examine the relationship of composers to society in terms of *patronage* and *poverty*. Interesting as this may be, we ought still to be aware of the clarity and intensity of particular works and to notice that the *same* social setting has often produced composers with strikingly *different* musical behaviours, and indeed that the same composer may make a range of musical objects, each quite different from the others. In other words, it is the relationship between human experience of life and the making of symbolic objects that is the prime location of aesthetic experience, not the social and historical context. This is why we can respond to music from many different cultures and historical times, in spite of the fact that we cannot possibly adopt those particular social, political or religious values. The meaningfulness and feelingfulness of music is not so confined.

We can now perhaps begin to see where music education so easily goes wrong and where we might put an emphasis to get things right.

The attempts we have been making to understand the fundamental musical and aesthetic processes may have generated enough light by which to see a way ahead. It is not so much a question of stopping bad educational practices but of starting better ones. We now have enough conviction and information to move forward more confidently towards that goal.

Music education is aesthetic education, which simply means that it cares for quality rather than quantity of experience. It seeks to promote vital responses to life and living, a sense of delight in all objects and events that come before us meaningfully, with clarity and power. The question before us now is the extent to which aesthetic attitudes can be *learned* and what the role of a teacher might be.

References

1. LAURENCE, I. (1977). 'The Composer's View of the Teacher', *Psychology of Music,* **5**, 2.
2. FINDLAY, J.W. (1968). *The Perspicuous and the Poignant: two aesthetic fundamentals.* In Osborne (Ed.) *Aesthetics in the Modern World.* Thames and Hudson.
3. WITKIN, R. (1974). *The Intelligence of Feeling.* Heinemann.
4. ROSS, M. (1978). *The Creative Arts.* Heinemann.

Chapter 4:

The Model in Action

We can now take up the threads of the previous sections and weave them together into a platform for action. In the first chapter we observed the inadequacy of several ways of regarding music: as direct sensuous pleasure; as organized sound; as a game people play; and as a kind of sound-picture language describing other things, stories, emotions and events in the lives of composers. In particular we drew an important distinction between sound materials and musical elements, a source of great confusion and misunderstanding at the roots of the theory and practice of music education. It is worth restating the crucial points again here and, in particular, the three vital processes that are brought to bear on sound materials by human thought and imagination.

Firstly the little bits of sound we use in music are *selected* from an enormous range of possibilities. In spite of the ideas of some *avant garde* composers, we do not accept any and all sounds as they happen to be emitted by a noisy world, and dub them music. Even on the level of ordinary perceptions, we select the sounds to which we will attend at any given moment. For example, I may be listening to what a friend is saying as we walk down a busy street and will push into the background of consciousness the noise of the traffic, although the roar of cars may be measurably louder than his voice. On the other hand, if we are crossing the road I might switch off attention to him and listen for approaching vehicles. As far as composers of music are concerned they select and reject sounds to some extent for us and draw our attention to this sound rather than that. This process of selection is in operation whatever the chosen sound materials might be, whether made by conventional musical instruments, electronic devices or 'collected' from 'life' on a tape-recorder. However, selection by itself will not give us music. After all, the boys of 3C select certain sounds to entertain the young lady student-teacher, but their motives are not musical and neither is the result.

Alongside with the selection of sound materials goes the process of *relating* sounds together. One sound may follow another or several sounds may be combined. Some sounds may be heard often and others more rarely, for example the 'normal' sound of the trombone and the whispered word 'Why?' in Berio's *Sequenza Five*. Tonality is a sound-relating system. In Indian music the stopped strings of the sitar make sounds in relationship with the unstopped strings just as in bagpipe music the chanter relates to the drone. However, even if sounds are both selected and related we do not necessarily have music as a result. At an underground station the squeal of brakes and the following hiss and thump of doors in the train is a sound relationship which we do not normally consider to be musical. Nor do we normally regard as music the sound of an orchestra tuning, although the pitch is selected and all the instruments are relating the pitch of their A's and other pitches to that of the oboe. (We may hear it as a promise of music to come, of course.)

The final ingredient of the spell that transforms sounds into music is the *intention* that there shall be music. It may be a composer, or a performer, or just a listener making his own music out of the sounds of train-wheels, but someone is intending music to happen. Just as the pumpkin and the mice are transformed into a coach and four, so our raw sounds cease to be aural materials and become charged with meaning to which we respond. And our response is an aesthetic response.

Unfortunately the word 'aesthetic' has fallen on hard times and tends to be ignored in discussion about music and music education in favour of more modish terms. Thus music is seen as a manifestation of creative self-expression, or a skill-learning activity, or as part of our cultural heritage. Music is, in part, all of these things and more, but they are not its central core. The reason for its existence in history and human culture, and the reason for the development of its special skills is that it affects the quality of life. Aesthetic means that we perceive and feel something and is not to be confused with 'ascetic', which means self-denying. An aesthetic experience is self-enriching. It is not necessarily something complicated and rarified or mystical and elusive. It is basically a response to something on its own terms and for the sake of what it means for us; a flower or a firework, a picture or a pop-song, an evocative word or the whole new world of a book. An aesthetic experience feeds the imagination and effects the way we feel about things: music without aesthetic qualities is like a fire without heat. We acknowledge the central importance of aesthetic qualities every time we say things like 'He has a good technique but his playing seems so insensitive and unmusical'. Skills alone are not enough.

I would suggest that a fundamental weakness in much teaching, and especially in general class music, lies in the failure to bring about any aesthetic response or even to notice that it is central to the situation. Skill acquisition and literature studies are so easily substituted for the prime activities of composition, audition and performance. Even when students are engaged in what is nominally composition and performance, it is still possible to miss the excitement of audition which should be embodied in these activities. So-called composition may be merely a random assembly of sound patterns, with little sense of selection, relation and intention, while performance may turn out to mean getting through something with technical control but without any vitality in communication or joy in response.

One reason for such shortcomings lies in the difficulties and confusions that entangle us when we leave the safe highway of skills and information. We noted in the second chapter that glib talk of music being 'self-expression' is not only highly ambiguous but often misleading. In the same way, loose descriptions of music somehow 'educating the emotions' are not very helpful and range from fairly crude ideas of catharsis to the notion of somehow training the emotions to behave themselves and submit to the proper control of reason. These diversions will certainly keep us from a proper understanding of music education as aesthetic education and it is obvious why many teachers avoid or react against them. Music is certainly not an activity set up in opposition to rational thought. On the contrary, it shares with logical thinking a foundation of human awareness, consciousness, or sentience. Music amongst the arts bridges the instinct and intellect, the affective elements of our experience and what we describe as 'rational'. Music is both feelingful *and* meaningful.

We also saw in Chapter 2 that the meaningfulness of music operates at two levels. We can be aware of the gestures of music, the ebbing and flowing of one feeling state into another, the clear attitudes, the ambiguous shadings and mergings, the fine details or grosser qualities of a musical object that have nothing to do with the identification of technical or historical features or of biographical or programmatic descriptions, and everything to do with our grasp of the stylistic norms within which the music operates. We know that in order to be motivated to continue to engage with music there must be a balance, within certain limits of tolerance, between novelty and the familiar, between the unexpected and expected, complexity and simplicity, foreground and background, deviations and norms, uncertainty and redundancy (Berlyne, 1974).[1]

We also know that beyond this there is a second level of meaning which is highly individual, a meaning embodied in the relationship a person has with any particular musical object. We may recognize the gestural *schemata* in music, may have our attention gripped in the tensions and resolutions generated by the inhibition or fulfilment of our expectations and yet remain unmoved and unimpressed by the work. It is as if we said of someone, 'I understand what you are saying and you say it in an interesting and engaging way, but I remain unconvinced and, to be honest, could not care less.' This would be a perfectly reasonable attitude and is one which we find ourselves in very often where music is concerned. It may mean something *to* us but little *for* us. Professional performers are often placed in the position of presenting works with which they have little sympathy and which elicit from them no profound response, yet they may present a work to an audience in a totally convincing and understanding manner, sufficient to permit the highest level of aesthetic response for the auditors. Similarly, we may, in the act of audition, stop short of this second level of meaning, where the music fuses many traces of our past experience together in a powerfully affective way, when we say we were 'moved'. This meaning 'embodied' and thus personalized in us is not to be had on demand and cannot be predicted. Consequently, nor can it be planned for in-teaching. Meaning 'for' can never form part of a syllabus, though we may always be looking for the signs that it happens in our students and delighted when we think we see them. Even in the act of composing we may not always aspire beyond the level of clarity to the intensity of image that we seek. We may be pleased with the work but not delighted; it may be craftsmanlike but not inspired; interesting but not enthralling.

This is not to denigrate the first level of aesthetic meaning, where the surface gestures of the music are understood, or to undervalue the importance of norm and deviation as motivating elements in an aesthetic situation. Far from it. These are the areas in which we *can* work, for which we *can* plan, through which we hope to see the development of aesthetic responsiveness in our students. Here are two prongs in the fork of precise objectives for music as aesthetic education. We might notice that the gestural aspect of music corresponds largely with expressive and *quasi* referential elements, while the relationship between the expected and the unexpected in music is the perceptible edge of its formal properties. Components of feeling (recognized through relative movement, weight, size, density and so on) are interlaced with structural features. To be exclusively a referentialist or a formalist is to be in error. We cannot hold them separate for long. We can, however, make each a starting point or the target of a specific objective in music education, briefly attending to one aspect rather than another. In so doing we are trying to develop *aesthetic appraisals*.

For example, we might want our students to identify the slow, dragging gait and drooping heaviness of the *St Louis Blues*. The words are at hand to help, should there be any doubt as to which area of feeling is presented at the first level of meaning. These would be the expressive elements. We may help them locate the change of words in the third line along with the accompanying faster rate of chord change. This need not be only at a level of aural skills but can be felt as an increase in complexity, as a deviation from the norms established in the first two lines, which is a way of holding our attention and motivating us to continue to engage with the music. It is true of course that this feature is a norm in 12-bar Blues tunes, but even so, one can continue to be slightly surprised by this formal element unless completely satiated. The 'riff' element during the second half of each line provides other opportunities for the performer to 'break' the pattern with improvised deviations. One does not have to say all this to be aware of it, but a teacher ought to know what possibilities there are for *feeling the form* as well as identifying the general mood. One strategy is to have the students imitate a simple basic Blues structure, gradually extending the range of improvised deviations without destroying the feeling character. All this is at the first level of meaning. But if a student should reveal that he begins to *enjoy* the sadness, to revel in the slow swing of the music (perhaps by the way he moves to it) then such a student is beginning to be engaged at the second level of meaning. Should someone then show signs of actively seeking out this kind of musical experience, then we can be fairly sure that this encounter with the Blues had aesthetic meaning for him. We can only proclaim this as a general aim. It cannot be specified as an objective, any more than we can specify that Jack should love Jill. All we can do is to see that Jack gets an opportunity to meet Jill properly.

We notice now that it is possible to formulate precise behavioural objectives to do with aesthetic appraisals. In the above example we did not say that we wanted the students to appreciate, like, or respond to the *St Louis Blues*. These words are vague, though often used in a well-intentioned way, and give us no clues as to what we might *do* to promote these desirable states and certainly no idea as to how we would know that it *was* appreciated. Instead we wanted our students to *identify* in this music a particular range of feeling. We were looking for them to *locate* the musical and verbal deviations in the third line and for them to *imitate* a simple Blues structure as a basis for improvisation. This in itself is a process of deviating from an understood norm. Involved at this level are the parameters of skill acquisition and literature studies. We shall have to make decisions about how far we may need to develop instrumental and aural skills during this project. These too can be specified in clear terms. For example, we might expect students to be able to invent 'riffs' using only four notes. Or we may want them to be able to recall certain specified information about the social and historical background of the Blues.

The cumulative effect of these activities is a form of analysis, or exploration of music. It is not just *doing* something but *acquiring* something through the doing, in terms of skills, concepts and attitudes. This point is well made by Reimer (1970, p.121).[2]

> The following words are suggestive of the many ways that musical exploration can take place: show, discuss, manipulate, imitate, compare, describe, define, identify, classify, modify, rearrange, reshape, vary, combine, contrast, develop, inspect, observe, amplify, reconstruct, characterize, infer, disclose, clarify, demonstrate, explain, appraise, discern, recall, locate, invent. All these shadings of exploration and many more one could add to the list can be described as the process of 'analyzing.' Analysis should not be thought of as the dry, sterile picking apart of the bare bones of music. Certainly it can be this and often is, especially in college music theory classes. Such 'analysis' would be the death of aesthetic education. When analysis is conceived as an active, involved exploration of the living qualities of music,

and when analysis is in constant and immediate touch with musical experience itself, it is the essential means for making musical enjoyment more obtainable.

There are great advantages in having specified clear objectives. Education is basically about *changing* people and we may as well be honest about this. All the time we are looking for changes in skill, attitudes and understanding, and especially for a growth of responsiveness to music. An objective is a prediction of change, God willing and with a following wind. Paradoxically, clear objectives give greater flexibility. We can employ a variety of strategies in our attempts to achieve them. The alternative is to fix on a particular activity and hope that something, if anything, comes out of it. All we know then is *how* the students are to be occupied, not *why*. If we are clear about *why* then we have no need to persist with an activity if it does not appear to be fruitful. We can change our tack, we can modify the objectives if necessary or abandon them entirely. They can be challenged by students and other teachers. Our cards are on the table. A vague commitment to an activity has none of these virtues. We cannot experiment with alternative forms of transportation if we do not know where we are going, nor can we decide on whether or not the journey is worth while in the first place. Furthermore, students will soon detect a lack of sense of direction if we cannot answer the question, 'why are we doing this?'.

One other feature to do with the setting up of clear objectives is that they contribute to the second main plank in any platform of music education. *Aesthetic experience* is the first principle; a sense of student (and teacher) *achievement* is the second. By 'achievement' we are not envisaging any formalized kind of testing or examination, but the positive pleasure we experience when we understand something, when we get something right or clear, when we master some element of skill, or find real enjoyment in an activity. We can only experience this accomplishment when the task is clearly defined and limited to highly specific items. A vague feeling of being more or less on the right lines is no substitute for the mastery of definite tasks within a lesson or practice session.

For the teacher, no less than the student, this is crucial. It promotes a feeling of progression and purpose in an activity, especially where there may be complex interrelating elements.

A teacher may formulate objectives in three main categories with the ultimate aim of aesthetic response in mind throughout. These areas form a hierarchy. The first is the category of aesthetic appraisals and involves the activities of *composition, audition and performance.* Here we are concerned with the quest for clarity of musical image, meaning 'to' and performance projection. The second area takes in *skill acquisition* and *literature studies.* The third is non-musical but is essential to any educational process, and may be called *human inter-action.* For example, it may be important to formulate objectives in the interests of promoting good relationships with students or between students, or give confidence to particular individuals. This category of objectives does not usually stand alone but is achieved through activities at the other levels. However, it may be that the teaching of music *per se* is sometimes abandoned for interpersonal reasons; for example, a class might be particularly difficult. If this is so then we ought at least to acknowledge it and look for ways of moving up the hierarchy whenever possible. Similarly, we would seek to move from skills and knowledge through to musical experience on an aesthetic level at every opportunity. Otherwise we are not engaged in music education in any meaningful sense of the term, though we might be concerned with other educational values.

There is an apparent paradox here in that aesthetic sharing can be one of the principles of human interaction. A mutual understanding between people, forged in a fire of enthusiasm for composition, audition or performance, is a strong bond indeed. In these situations music functions *instrumentally* as a focus for friendship along with any other activity that can be shared. In this way it can confer great benefits, both socially and in the field of music therapy. However, this is not the *intrinsic* aesthetic core of musical experience, though instrumental aims may be valued just as highly or higher at times than aesthetic purposes. Fundamentally, aesthetic education has to do with the relationship between a person and an aesthetic object or event. Other people may or may not be concerned in this relationship and at the high points of response tend to recede into the background. In fact, they can be a nuisance with their coughing and comments. No doubt at times we are helped in audition by being part of an audience, communally attentive and focused in unison on the same unfolding object that is before us. But at times a solitary exploration is both sufficient and necessary, a private discovery of the forms of feeling that resonate in art objects.

The point is that we are concerned here with a hierarchy of values for *music education,* not for education in general. In such a hierarchy interpersonal relationships and human interactions are necessary but never sufficient conditions under which we formulate our teaching objectives. In order to play our role in the general processes of education we need to be sure of our *specific* contribution and the particular emphasis on our concerns. We do not need to claim that we are educating the 'whole person', only that we offer something distinctive and significant for the growth and development of human beings. With this in mind we can now outline our hierarchy of objectives areas.

AN OBJECTIVES HIERARCHY

Ultimate aim – aesthetic response
Intensity of image in composition
Meaning 'for' during audition
Sense of impact in performance

This cannot be predicted or taught for, though it might be 'caught' from another person. In terms of achievement, the student should be able to seek out aesthetic encounters for their intrinsic qualities.

CATEGORY I
Aesthetic appraisals
Clarity of image in composition
Meaning 'to' during audition
Projection in performance

General Formulations
The student should be able to . . .
(a) recognize and produce in music a range of expressive gesture
(b) identify and display the operation of norms and deviations

CATEGORY II
Skill acquisition

Literature studies

The student should be able to . . .
(c) demonstrate aural discriminations, technical fluency, use of notations
(d) assemble and categorize information about music and musicians

CATEGORY III
Human interaction

The student should be able to . . .
cooperate with others and find pleasure in shared experiences

This overview is helpful in several ways. For example, we might ask why we seem to be spending most time with activities intended to strengthen Category III. If real music teaching is not possible we should say so, and look for help in other directions. It may be that our way of working is inappropriate, or that the level of material is wrong, or that the students are disturbed by the personality of the teacher, or that they are a group badly adjusted to school, or whatever the institution. (This might also suggest that the institution is badly adapted to the students!) This last situation is fairly common in some urban schools especially. Solutions are required that are more radical than tampering with a curriculum and are certainly beyond the control of any individual teacher.

Far more common though, is the case where time and energy are devoted almost exclusively to functioning in Category II. Why does this happen? Is it because we have no proper theory of music education? Or because this is how we were taught? Or because we ourselves are not aesthetically aware? Whatever the reason, it is all too rare to find teaching backed up by the belief that objectives in Category II are only instrumental to achieving objectives in Category I. Objectives in both categories should run side by side, skills and knowledge supporting and facilitating aesthetic appraisals through the activities of composition, audition and performance.

One important side-effect of working across the C(L)A(S)P parameters is that our students may become more flexible and open in the roles they play with regard to music and, consequently, may see more human possibilities in one another and the teacher. Oddly enough then, by setting out as though we were not directly concerned with aspects of human interaction we end by improving the position in Category III. And this is what we would expect: after all we do not become happy by *trying* to be happy and we do not always improve human relations by *looking* at one another but by *doing* something together that feels worthwhile. For this reason, the objectives given in the following, detailed samples of C(L)A(S)P in action are located in the first two categories only. In any case, we could not begin to formulate any precise objectives in the area of human interaction unless we knew the particular humans concerned!

We will begin by looking at some examples from general music classes in school, for it is here that great difficulties are often experienced. No specification has been given concerning age and previous experience of the students. Judgements about what is or is not possible at particular ages and stages will vary from school to school and teacher to teacher. We can say only that similar objectives and activities have been explored with groups of children between the ages of ten and fourteen.

The activities are taken more or less at random and are not sequential. They are not necessarily 'lessons'. A series of 'lessons' could be evolved from any one of these starting-points. There are endless variations on themes of this kind. The fundamental requirements are always the same: the teacher must be a *musician* in the strongest and widest sense of the term, but must also be a *'teacher'*, a professional, able to predict and work for specific outcomes of student achievement. With this in mind, precise objectives are stated relating to aesthetic appraisals through composition, audition and performance, and to skill acquisition and literature studies (Categories I and II). We are thus involved with the four general formulations given in the hierarchy but articulated in detail for particular educational settings. We might remind ourselves of these general formulations:

The student should be able to . . .

1. Recognize and produce in music a range of expressive gesture.
2. Identify and display the operation of norms and deviations.
3. Demonstrate aural discriminations, technical fluency, use of notations.
4. Assemble and categorize information about music and musicians.

We can now go forward, bearing in mind that there may be countless other *unspecified* outcomes. The main thing is that we are setting out purposefully.

Sample activities

Objectives The students should be able to recognize and respond to events in music that surprise us by contradicting our expectations. They should also be able to compose and perform a small-scale piece of music that embodies a surprise.

Resources required Three contrasting groups of instruments are to be positioned in separated parts of the room; for example, a cluster of 'white' note chime bars, a group of 'black' note chime bars, and a collection of non-pitched instruments.

Strategy The teacher has each group separately play quietly to make a non-metric sound texture, starting and ending at a signal (This is the (S) part of C(L)A(S)P.) A signal to one group means that the other groups should *not* play.

The teacher then 'composes' and the class performs a piece that in notation might look like this. The only notation in use though is the agreed signal.

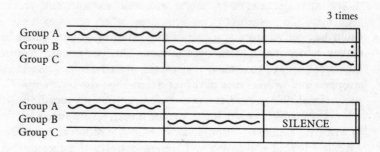

We ought to be surprised by something *not* happening. Group C does not play at the end and this breaks up the established pattern.

It is not hard to find a piece of recorded music where this kind of surprise takes place. For example, the jazz pianist Jelly Roll Morton has on record a number called *The Crave*. If we listen to this, tapping or clicking along with the beat, we shall find ourselves surprised by two patches of silence near the end. The beat goes on but the sound stops. The effect is something like being thrown forward when a car stops suddenly. It is the biggest surprise in an engaging piece of music full of little deviations (syncopations) from the repeated beat. To feel the playfulness and humour of this is to respond in an aesthetic way, it is a true act of audition.

Once again we might rehearse and perform a short composition, though this time with notation. Each measure is ten seconds long.

What kind of surprise do we have here? We are led to expect fairly long sound durations, but groups B and C give us short sounds. The order of instruments is also changed. It seems that surprises happen when a *contrast* breaks up a *repeated* pattern. We might think of other ways of setting up and breaking patterns – changes of volume, of pitch, of metre and of timbre.

If possible, small groups of five or six students might now work out their own compositions for voices and instruments, short pieces containing some form of surprise. Eventually, these will be performed to the rest of the pupils as auditors.

At some stage we could play a recording of Greig's second *Norwegian Dance*. This surprises us by breaking off very suddenly in the middle section and returning, without any apparent reason, to the first idea.

We ought to be clear that we are not playing a record to illustrate a compositional device but to provoke a response, to set up a framework for listening that makes it possible to *feel* something, in this case a particular quality of surprise. Nor are we concerned primarily to introduce students to the music of Greig or Jelly Roll Morton or anyone else. Our objective is the recognition of and response to musical events of a certain kind and we are working towards it through composition, audition and performance. We have also to attend to certain skills, the discipline of playing together and quietly, in watching signals and translating notation into action. We may indeed want to give some information about music heard on record, indulging (briefly) in literature studies, but this will usually be *after* the event. Psychologically it is so much stronger to come to a musical object with something definite in mind, in this instance the concept of surprise, than to say 'Now we are going to listen to a piece of music by . . . who was born in . . . , wrote so many symphonies, etc. etc.' Who cares? We may wish to know this kind of thing if we find some quality of experience in the music that excites or pleases us. Otherwise it is simply inert information that may even function in a negative way, in that people will avoid exposing themselves to what they may rightly regard as incomprehensible and boring experiences attached to names like Beethoven or Boulez. The experiences only become comprehensible and interesting if we hold some kind of mental key to them. The concept of surprise is merely one such key. First we enjoy the cake, then we might ask where we can buy some more.

There will, of course, be times where literature studies are both desirable and necessary, but we need to ask, does the knowledge about a composer, a work, or a musical period enhance and enrich subsequent experiences of audition. For example, some idea of expectations within a sonato form may help us perceive more acutely and respond more profoundly to the particular qualities of the work in question. But even here it seems that such preparation might well be based on audition and listening skills developed on shorter pieces in a binary structure, in order to feel the main swing of the music away from the tonic and back to it. A development section is then heard as even more of a deviation away from the tonic and the material of the opening, and powerful expectations are set up for the return of the first key centre and first subject. The GCE question, asking what is unusual about the last movement of Beethoven's *Eighth Symphony* can only be properly answered if students have some concept of what is *usual* in such a movement, and this requires not only information about musical forms, but substantial experience of other works.

Reactions in Music

Objectives The students should be able to work from a limited form of notation; identify aggressive and submissive reactions between musical events; respond imaginatively to a contemporary work involving reactions of this kind.

Resources required The following notational vocabulary is displayed on a board.

(1)	**(3)**
t . . . . (repeated)	ss (soft)
(2) k (loud)	**(4)** SILENCE

Strategy The class is divided into two equal groups. Each of the four units is rehearsed. None of the consonants are 'voiced' except the 'k'. One group now assumes responsibility for units 1 and 2, the other for 3 and 4. Each group has a leader or conductor who will indicate with a hand raised high or low which of the two units is to be performed. The leader of the second group will wait until the first group has made some kind of musical statement using the two available sounds and then respond with permutations of units 3 and 4. Trial and error, discussion and rehearsal ought to shape a piece of music in which group A, with the more aggressive sounds, dominates group B or, alternatively, is eventually silenced by the persistance of group B. This composition might be recorded so that the class can hear how it sounds from the point of view of auditors, whether or not the ideas are clear and the impact strong. If not, we might try again.

Two pieces of music on record immediately spring to mind. Berio's *Visage* contains a passage where the human voice reacts to electronically produced sounds through a whole range of feelings; doubt, wonder, fear, terror, dismay. More traditionally, the slow movement of Beethoven's *Fourth Piano Concerto* shows an interaction of firmness in the orchestral strings with the quiet solo piano. There may also be the possibility of playing a recording of another class tackling the same problem.

Exactly at what stage the work of professional composers should be presented will depend on many things. In certain situations it may be helpful to show how someone else handled particular ideas before the students make their own attempts. This could, on the other hand, be confusing or off-putting and it is probably best to hold back on professional recordings until they really do seem appropriate. We may have more insight into such works as a result of our own endeavours. It is not being suggested that we offer the contributions of acknowledged composers in the spirit of 'look what a real composer does'. There may indeed be more sympathy with and a sharper response to the home-grown product. The important thing is that clear musical concepts are being formed and sensitivities developed through activities across the five musical parameters and over a range of musical styles.

Objectives The students should be able to recognize and control changes of timbre when the pitch remains stable; they should understand that this can be an expressive musical device.

Resources required Instruments that sustain sound.

Strategy If the class sings reasonably well and can sustain a chord in tune then the triad of Bb major can be divided amongst the class, one note to each of three separate groups (in the lower octave). Each group is to keep its note going, individually breathing at random, resting where necessary, but always enough voices to carry the note. The chord of Bb is then the fixed element. So far it is a matter of skill acquisition, nothing more. But now each group can be directed to sing loudly or softly or, by using closed and open hand hand-signs, to vary the vocal colour from 'eeh' to 'aah'. A group may stop altogether. The effect will be of a stationary object (pitch) with changing light and shade and colour. We get a similar experience when watching trees and buildings in a sunset, or hedges by the light of a bonfire and fire-works, or some neon advertising signs. Different members of the class might try to compose pieces using these limited resources and hand-signs.

Now we have some concept of timbre or colour change we might listen to part of *Stimmung* by Stockhausen. Here are similar materials in a slowly evolving work, though after several minutes other events take place, such as spoken words and repeated vowels, still in the context of the sustained chord.

Instruments can be substituted for voices. Melodicas, harmonicas and string instruments will be especially useful, though wind and possibly pitched percussion could be brought in. The aim now is to find ways of exploiting the range of colour mixes on the available instruments, not only in the centre of notes but also ways of starting and stopping the sound. The use of silence, surprise, reactions, may help to give interest to the emerging compositions, but the natural tendency will be to feel a quality of stillness, brought about by the stationary chord, with sparks of activity around it.

This particular formal device is not confined to composers of the twentieth century. Purcell has a *Fantasy Upon One Note* for strings, where one part (the tenor) holds and repeats middle C. The opening of Wagner's *Das Rheingold* is the long and famous passage built on the chord of Eb. Bach especially loves to lay down 'pedal points' as a pitch norm against which the other lines strain and to which harmonic centre they return after their deviations. Music based on drones from Scotland and India exemplifies the same principle in action – a fixed pitch norm against which another part strives to deviate and to which it usually succumbs.

The use of drones is very possible in general music classes, especially if people can work in smaller groups. Half a group maintains the drone while the others take turns in inventing variation, starting with the drone pitch, moving away, and returning, or perhaps *not* returning but teasing the auditor right to the end. Different groups may have different materials selected for them or make their own choices. One group might have a pentatonic series through which to deviate from the lowest note; another might have the first five notes of a major scale; another the first half of a minor scale; another could have six notes of a chromatic scale; and yet another may use the sliding and micro-tuned series possible on a string instrument or a 'Swanee whistle'. With this experience behind them it is much less likely that students will find the introductory section in Indian ragas (the *alap*) so strange or incomprehensible. That it tends to be so is an indication that in such passages the norms are not perceived and, consequently the deviations go by *unfelt* as playfulness or tension. Such music is highly formal, making its impact on us through structural relation-ships rather than expressive gestures. (In an Indian raga improvisation these are felt later on in the evolution of the music, especially when the *tabla* begins to play and strong rhythmic elements are set up. These we *can* feel as gestural experiences referring them to our muscles and body postures.)

Here again our objectives can be precise: the student should be able to control a free part in relation to a drone, demonstrating tension and resolution within the relationship and recognizing these properties in an Indian raga. These are limited and reasonable goals. If we succeed in helping people towards them we ought to be pleased. We should, of course, be delighted if students wanted to compose, hear and perform more of this kind, especially if it seemed that they were genuinely responsive in an aesthetic way. However, as we observed earlier, we cannot predict and teach directly towards the development of aesthetic response, but only make sure that we are always working towards aesthetic *recognition*. We are in the position of leading horses to water. Whether they drink or not is really their affair. But at least we can make sure that it is to water we are going, and not to a history of wells, or the analysis of H_2O, or learning how the word 'water' is written, or hearing from more learned horses, their opinions as to the value of one water hole compared with another.

Even so, some teachers may object that even the limited objectives we have set ourselves here will be beyond their students. But is this so? Is it really so difficult to sustain *one* note on an instrument or group of instruments? Is it very much more difficult for an individual to move away from that note to one another and back again? Could we not then reasonably expect that a spiral of increasing adventurousness be embarked upon, even if our limits are up to, say, three notes? We may well feel the need to develop aural discriminations of pitches during these processes and to initiate a discussion about notes that *match* and notes that *collide* with the drone. But let us not underestimate the musical ability and responsiveness of most students. They are often able to recognize and perform from a substantial and changing repertoire of pop songs without apparent effort, merely because they are motivated to repeat and repeat again exposure to the musical items. So it is in these strategies. By composing, attentively listening, and performing; by working at relevant skills and assimilating relevant knowledge, aesthetic appraisals can be developed and the doors opened a little wider to the possibility of aesthetic response.

We might consider just one more example from the school classroom. This involves the development of some traditional notation skills, though not the 'theory' of notation divorced from its use. In this example we shall not be starting something new but moving forward from previously achieved objectives. We assume that most of the group can distinguish between *me* and *doh*, the third degree and the degree of the tonic of a major scale. By 'distinguish' we mean that when one is sung or played after the other, the students can recognize the order in which they appear. In order to be sure of this we must have some kind of labels; *sol-fa*, note names, numbers 3 and 1. Or we might be asking which one of these patterns they hear.

Most of these students (we are assuming) can go beyond recognition and *read* patterns like this, singing them accurately in any order.

We now come to another stage in the process.
Objectives The student should be able to discriminate between pitch patterns made from the first three notes of a major scale; read the patterns (singing) in different orders; vary order, speed and volume to express different feeling gestures; and follow the effect of one pattern as it appears in the texture of an orchestral piece.
Resources required The following notational vocabulary is displayed.

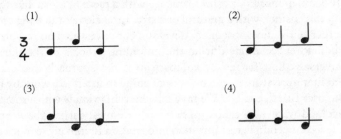

Strategy The teacher might ask if the first fragment can be sung at sight and what is new about patterns 2, 3 and 4. These will then be sung to the students to establish the sound of the second degree of the scale in relation to the others. The students may then be asked to recognize the order in which the patterns are sung and played to them, for example, 1,2,3,4. The students can then practice each unit and sing them in various combinations as indicated by a 'conductor'. To give a stronger sense of phrase and line, in other words to move from mere skill acquisition to performance, words such as the following may be sung to any four patterns in combination.

Over the quiet fields

Ring out the sound of bells

Students will have suggestions about the possibilities of different orders (composition) and especially concerning the effect of *repeating* a pattern, for example, 4,4,3,4. Once again, we are handling the essentials of norm and deviation, of repetition and contrast, but on a small scale. We can also explore the (limited) possibilities for different kinds of gesture by playing with the variables of speed and loudness. For example, 1,1,1,1, sung fast and loud will be quite different in expressiveness from 3,3,3,3, performed slowly and quietly. This may require the invention of new words. In the first instance the effect may be felt as jerky, angular, mechanical: in the second it could be smooth, flowing (if sung *legato*) and gentle. Can we invent suitable words for these? Now, taking pattern 3 in the key of E Major, we can become auditors to Bizet's *Carillon* from *L'Arlesienne*. The figure is repeated over and over again, against another melody, disappearing in the middle section but returning by stealth before the return of the opening idea. The teacher might help arouse expectations here by saying that it may come back, but when and how could be a surprise.

It is much more powerful to engage with a piece of music like this, from the 'inside', with a gestural or a structural element to hang on to in order to *feel* any subsequent development of gesture and be able to formulate expectations during the unfolding process of the music. Conversely, how barren by comparison is the approach that starts from literature studies – 'Now we are going to listen to a work by the composer Bizet', etc. etc. We may indeed want to know who wrote the piece and what it is called. (The words we used earlier about bells make a connection here.) But such information is unlikely to motivate us to attend to the music and might be off-putting for students who are suspicious of names like Bizet.

Where might we go from here? There are many possibilities. The skills so far acquired can be used to read this beautiful three-note tune from Wales (starting on A.)

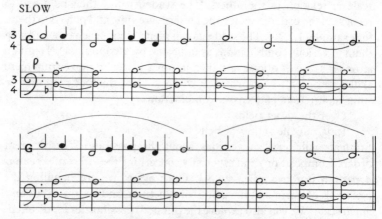

The simple lower parts could go to various instruments. We might add other lines to our stave, extending it gradually to five lines, but only as we need them for reading and only as we can cope with them. We could follow through the possibilities for composition with whatever pitch control is achieved. We may want to explore *Carillon* a little further, the orchestration, the levels of volume, the other themes, or more of the music of Bizet in the collection from *L'Arlésienne*. We are certainly not averse to literature studies provided they know their place!

We can look back over these few examples noticing a fairly wide range of music and constant movement from one area of C(L)A(S)P to another: yet the learning experiences need not be fragmentary. The activities are held together by the direction imparted through the specification of clear and precise objectives. We might also notice that we have not spoken of students being 'creative' (though they have composed), or limited ourselves to contemporary music (though we have included it), or forced any kind of subject integration (though we have worked with the concept of 'colour', and, in a small way, functioned as poets). These are issues requiring more careful attention and form the substance of the following chapter.

Once the C(L)A(S)P way of working is properly assimilated there is no limit to its possibilities, though this is no place to give more examples in detail. It is much more important to grasp the structure and style of thinking. Then we may apply it to our own specific situations. If we hear *any* piece of music we simply ask, does it feel good, what are its outstanding characteristics? Can these be handled by students in practical terms as composition and performance, is there a chance that this work might find a response in our students as auditors? How can we prepare for this by establishing the central concepts that underpin understanding of the musical behaviour of the work? Alternatively, we may have a fairly good idea of the skills of students in a class. Can we use these in a musical rather than a mechanical way? For example, a group of recorder players can play three notes: what we now need is a number of good *tunes* for performance within those limitations and the stimulation to improvise (compose) with the same scraps of sound material. Or again, at a choral or orchestral rehearsal we might ask whether, at any time, we are concerned merely with skills, or is there a sense of performance; whether the works chosen are so demanding in the skill areas as to obliterate any chance of the performance feeling, let alone involved audition among those who listen. Or, conversely, whether the performance that *might* be possible is inhibited by lack of attention to specific skills in rehearsal, or that some more careful study of the literature is required to give the performance a stylistic focus.

I hope enough has been said to hint at the possibilities of C(L)A(S)P as a framework for thinking and action in music education. However simple or complex the activity, in whatever musical style, in any age or social setting, the fundamental principles remain the same. Are we really trying to organize CAP or are we merely content to stay with (L) and (S)? Are we happy just to occupy students or does it matter *how* they are occupied, what skills, concepts and attitudes are being developed? Can we formulate precise objectives? If we can become clearer about these things we may find that music teaching not only becomes more purposeful but also more musical.

References
1. BERLYNE, D.E. (1974). *Studies in the New Experimental Aesthetics*. Hemisphere Publications: USA.
   See also MEYER, L. (1965). *Emotion and Meaning in Music*. Chicago.
2. REIMER, B. (1970). *A Philosophy of Music Education*. Prentice-Hall, New Jersey.
On formulating objectives the following may be found illuminating:
BLOOM, B.S. (Ed) (1956). *Taxonomy of Educational Objectives*, Book 2. Longmans, Green and Co., New York.
MAGER, R.F. (1975, 1962). *Preparing Instructional Objectives*. Fearon Publishers, USA.

Chapter 5

'Creativity', 'Contemporary' and 'Integration'

Creativity

To engage in a discussion of creativity with colleagues in music education is to embark on a slippery road indeed. Notions of self-expression, self-fulfilment, self-awareness; insistence on the necessity of being creative in today's society; suggestions that creative activities are the royal road to really understanding music; all these and many other claims are made for creativity. It is a fairly vague word. It is also an *approval* word. It is thought to be good to be creative or to promote creative activities, not so good to be non-creative, merely a performer or receiver of other people's creations. The issue is made all the more confusing by the use of the term 're-creative' to describe performance activities, a term which has some connection with recreation. Above all, creativity is a *vogue* word. One sees advertisements for creative salesmen, or creative holidays. A concert review once described a conductor as creative. Neville Cardus, in an obituary, was described as 'a creative critic'. Some people are called creative in a general way, others not. The term has crept into use in almost every area of life. At an international airport I picked up a book entitled *Creative Divorce*! I would say that a misunderstanding and misuse of this term can not only cause conceptual confusion but also lead to inadequate practice in teaching, and it is therefore very necessary to examine the term more carefully and, in a less emotive kind of way than is often the case.

I shall begin this examination by looking at some of the contributions made by psychologists to the creativity debate. We notice first the influential work of Carl Rogers who maintains that there is a great social need for creative individuals. According to Rogers (1970), our culture suffers from a 'dearth of creativity', as follows.[1]

Our formal education in schools and elsewhere tends to produce conformists, stereotypes, rather than 'original' people. In leisure-time activities, entertainment is received passively and often in large groups instead of being individually creative. In the sciences and in industry there are relatively few original people coming up with new ideas and hypotheses. Even in individual and family life we have a strong tendency to conform in dress, food, ideas and so on. Rogers insists that in our age knowledge is bounding along at an incredible speed, and as a consequence of this 'genuinely creative adaptation seems to represent the only possibility that man can keep abreast of the kaleidoscopic change in his world'. The consequences of failing to promote creativity, according to Rogers, are dire. 'Not only individual maladjustment and group tensions but international annihilation will be the price we pay for a lack of creativity.' Here then is the great *social* need for creative individuals. The successful evolution of mankind requires rapid change and adaptation in human attitudes, skills, knowledge and awareness. We need to proceed by creative leaps in order to cope successfully with the future. Other psychologists, especially Anthony Storr (1976), have argued that creative behaviour is also an answer to a *personal* need.[2] Storr's interesting thesis is that there is something 'intrinsically frustrating about human infancy'. As infants we want to do and be things we are just not able to achieve. We are, in many ways, at the mercy of parents and other people, often experiencing severe disturbance and anxiety through the frustrations created by constraints imposed on us by parents, society and our own immaturity, lack of skills, knowledge and the power to influence the world about us. As a result, we develop an inner world, a world of phantasies, trying to satisfy our desires and gratify the needs we have. Creative people, says Storr, are those who are particularly affected in a powerful way by this experience of infancy, and later on in life they develop ways of externalizing these phantasies in works of art, scientific ideas, literature and so on. On this view creativity is a way of dealing with deep personal problems. Its development is necessary to individual health and well-being, not only to social needs in our technological, high-speed society.

A great deal of work in psychology has proceeded by trying to identify the factors or traits which make up creative behaviour. The rationale behind this is that if we can identify the particular items of human behaviour that make up creative actions, we may better be able to promote these in education. One well-known criterion is that creative behaviour tends to be *divergent*, that is to say, not moving in a straight line or predictable way but leaping from possibility to possibility in new ways, seeing connections between previously separate entities. The creative person is, therefore, more like a taxi able to weave in and out of traffic, take side turnings, change direction and cope with diversions, as opposed to non-creative behaviour which would be more like a railway train fixed in direction by the existing lines of the track. This idea of divergence has been expressed in many different ways. Arthur Koestler calls it 'bisociation'. Edward De Bono calls it 'lateral thinking'. Basically this means that we break out of the rut of received ideas and gain new insights.

Other items listed as making up creative behaviour have been identified by a number of writers. For example, Guilford (1970) gives fluency, flexibility, originality, sensitivity to problems, redefinition of problems and elaboration.[3] Burt (1962) gives fluency, divergence, insight and receptivity.[4] Fluency we might define as a fast rate or flow of ideas. The notion of flexibility resembles that of divergence. It involves the ability to switch from one area or field of knowledge to another, to make new relationships. Originality most people would take as being axiomatic to any idea of creativity, though we should notice that there has been considerable discussion as to whether a creative person needs to be original in terms of producing something absolutely new or merely new for the *individual* concerned. The most recent view is that creativity is a kind of 'spiritual energy'. What really matters is that an individual makes a creative leap for him or herself whether or not it is new in any absolute sense (Elliott, 1971).[5] Guilford's 'sensitivity to problems', however, suggests more than this and resembles Burt's 'insight'. Creative action is selective. It isn't just applied to any old problem, but to those problems that are important and have useful consequences through being solved. If this is considered an important trait of creativity then presumably we would doubt the true creativeness of a person who invented novel but useless and worthless objects whatever the level of his 'spiritual energy'. The concept of 'redefinition' seems similar to that of 'receptivity'. Here, the creative person sees the familiar in a new way and redefines old problems in fresh terms that make them capable of solution. Finally, by 'elaboration' is meant the ability to sustain the development of an idea and to follow it through. It is not left half baked.

Some psychologists consider that these ideas are often misunderstood and tend to result in some doubtful assumptions. Hudson (1966) identifies certain 'influential, imprecise and often misleading views', that the conventional intelligence test is out of date, that we should instead have tests of creativity, that creativeness is personal rather than intellectual, that the diverger is always the creative person and that convergence is a form of neurotic defence.[6]

I mention these things briefly in order that we should be aware of a great deal of research, writing and discussion that has taken place on the concept of creativity long before and during recent discussion of it in terms of music education. We could, it seems to me, save ourselves a lot of time and misunderstanding if we took the trouble to go to the sources of the ideas which are so casually and haphazardly employed in our own deliberations. At least we might think more carefully about what we really mean. For example, can we really assume that creative people are well-adjusted by virtue of their creativeness. The typical picture of the romantic artist or musician suggests the opposite, a high state of tension which rarely seems to be resolved. Indeed, the sheer activity of creating may promote considerable disturbance and sometimes be avoided because of this. In his marvellous memoirs, Hector Berlioz tells us that he dreamt one night of a new symphony, but on waking he dismissed the possibility of going to write down the ideas because he would involve himself in the labour of copying it, the cost of performing it and financial problems caused by being unable to carry out other work, such as writing articles. On the second night after this he again heard the symphony in a dream and even seemed to see it written down.[7]

> I woke in a state of feverish excitement, I hummed the theme to myself; its form and character pleased me exceedingly. I was on the point of getting up. Then my previous thoughts recurred and held me fast. I lay still, steeling myself against temptation, clinging to the hope that I would forget . . . 'Coward!'. Some young fanatic will say (I forgive him in advance for his discourtesy). You should have taken the risk! You should have written it down! You should have ruined yourself!

This is all right as far as it goes, but are the workings of the mind of a particularly eccentric genius in any way to be compared with the activities of children in school? Wallach and Kogan (1965) suggest there is evidence to suppose that this might indeed be the case.[8] When they attempted to measure levels of anxiety, intelligence and creativity in children at school, they found the least anxious children were those with high I.Qs and low scores on creativity. There were higher levels of anxiety amongst children with high creativity scores. It seems unlikely that being creative is necessarily a passport to a land of good adjustment, happiness, and freedom from stress. Indeed, the reverse may sometimes be true.

We ought now to consider the idea of creativity as it more directly concerns music education.

During the early 1970s, long after its appearance on the scene of art and drama education, the concept of creativity thrust its way into the foreground of thinking and practice in music education. Courses for teachers of music were set up with the word central to their titles; teachers became converted to the kinds of activities that marched under its banner; commercially-interested parties, such as publishers and the makers of musical instruments, slipped it into advertisements. Expressions like 'creative work' and 'creative music' were employed without qualification or explanation, since it was assumed that their meaning is clear and generally accepted. And to a certain extent this is so, in that some particular activities in the field of school music seemed to attract a consensus opinion that they were 'creative'. My concern here is to draw out the implied conditions that make for 'creativity' in music and to offer criticism of the degree of exclusiveness that crept into its usage and still lingers on, and of the neglect of other aspects relating to a broader concept of 'creativity'.

Perhaps it could be generally agreed that what Sinnott (1959) calls 'the great gift of imagination' is essential to the concept.[9]

> Hence must have come the use of fire, communication by written symbols, the invention of the wheel and the bow, domestication of animals, and many more . . . they were all novelties that could not have appeared unless there had been someone who could imagine a situation never yet experienced, who could picture in his mind something he had not seen.

The manipulation of images to come to some new idea, to have a new experience or to make a new object of some kind seems central, and with regard to music education 'creative' and 'imaginative' are sometimes used interchangeably and are always closely linked.

A second string to this bow of 'creativity' would be that people should make up their own music, rather than merely performing or passively listening to the music of others.

The phrase 'creative music' is here taken to have two aspects:

through experiment children may discover the nature of sounds improvise their own music either individually or in groups; or they may take an existing melody and make an original arrangement of it for voices and instruments. (Department of Education and Science, 1970)[10]

We might notice two things at this point. Firstly, there are sound general educational principles involved here which take into account the close relationship between doing and knowing and the requirements of stimulating pupil motivation and interest. Secondly, though, the incorporation of this factor into the concept of 'creativity' begins to exclude certain activities which might well be taken in under the heading of 'imaginative'. I am thinking of the performance of music composed by other people, which, I intend to argue later, may have the right to be considered to involve 'creative' elements.

A third strand recently woven into the 'creative' concept is an emphasis on non-tonal and non-metric music, often that of *avant garde*. More conventional and skill-intensive techniques are subordinated to a freer use of percussion instruments, electronically-modified or produced-sounds, and unusual effects from sound sources not previously regarded as musical: 'The sound materials and improvisatory procedures being explored in creative music in schools reproduce many of the ideas of some adult contemporary composers ...' (Schools Council, 1972).[11] 'Children now compose and improvise pieces in groups in a number of schools and absorb much of the idiom of modern music without formal instruction.' (Self, 1967).[12]

Here again, if such a condition is to be taken as essential to 'creative' activities, everything is excluded except certain contemporary styles, though no one, when pressed, would insist that music-making in other styles may not be just as 'creative'. In current practice, however, the contemporary music bias is very evident.

This emphasis on contemporary music is understandable. It can easily be assumed that the music of our own time reflects the concerns and preoccupations of the present and should therefore be an important area, perhaps the most important area of activity for students today.

From a lineage extending from the Baroque orchestra and contrapuntal forms of the sixteen hundreds through the orchestral sounds and musical concepts of the nineteenth century, to the electronic, complex and dissonant music of today, one can trace the nature of man's sensitivity to a changing environment.

(Manhattanville Music Curriculum Program, 1970)[13]
The consequence of this is that:

> The materials of instruction must be drawn from the total
> spectrum of the art with primary emphasis on the materials of
> music today. For the strongest bond between the musical art and
> the student is sensitivity to contemporary life.

This is a powerful argument and a clear statement of the case, and it
is certainly true that a great deal of music teaching in schools and
colleges has emphasized the opposite, the curatorial or museum aspect
of music composed in the past and often over-reverently presented in
the present. Christopher Small (1977) believes that we need to
actually reject the 'classics', to be free of the narrow view of music
surrounding them and certainly to be very wary about valuing the
notation in which they are encoded as a central part of music
education.[14] We also need to approach the 'masterworks' without 'the
intervention of musicologists'. This is a view with which one can have
a great deal of sympathy. However, we ought to notice that the music
of today for most people is *not* what is known as contemporary music
but can be found under the umbrella term 'pop music', a phrase
covering a multitude of sins and virtues. Yet pop is often regarded
with suspicion, or at least avoided by those advocating contemporary
music as a basis for contemporary music education. It is possible that,
in some instances, activities in school which are strongly linked to
particular *avant garde* techniques may be seen by students to be yet
another special brand of 'school music', without relationship to the
radio or other aspects of the media encountered at home and elsewhere. This state of affairs requires careful and imaginative handling,
involving not only the education of children but also of parents. For
example, in one school known to the writer, there are frequent
parents' evenings when adults can actually hear live and recorded
performances of children's compositions along with relevant works by
internationally-known composers. This may indeed help to prevent
the separation of music in schools from music in the community,
though it seems to be an isolated situation.

At this point we can with profit return yet again to C(L)A(S)P.
Contemporary music, when we play the role of composer (C) may well
involve contemporary techniques and styles. But what about the role
of auditor (A)? I would suggest that contemporary music for the
auditor is not necessarily the music that is *composed* today but the
music that is *available* today, the music which comes to us via the

pressing of a button, going to the cinema or to concerts or folk clubs or discos and so on. On this definition contemporary music includes the music of other cultures and sub-cultures, including pop. Not only does the definition reach out laterally and ethnically in this way but also vertically into history, back into time, including the 'classics', but going back beyond them to mediaeval music, in fact as far as scholars can unearth the remains of older musics from other times. Indeed, we are in a unique and novel situation at present. Research and technology between them make our position totally different from any previous time in man's development. Older composers and auditors had access mainly to music of their time or just before (think of Bach, for example), and to very little of that. We, the moderns, can summon up voices from the past and far abroad with ease. Indeed, they often appear without a summons. We might in one day encounter, by accident or design, music from four centuries and ten cultures.

Looking at what it means to handle contemporary music in this light, it seems clear that the primary emphasis should be not so much on 'the materials of music today' in the narrow sense but in the wider. Our task is surely to enlarge the areas of 'responsiveness', to develop in ourselves and others an attentive and caring attitude to the myriad musics that surround us. If 'integration' means anything at all it is that each individual makes sense of his world and relates positively and actively to the various elements of human experience. The materials of today are not all being made today: we are also *inheritors*.

The last condition for 'creativity' that I would pick out as being fairly widely accepted is the notion of 'integration'. This is another of those hazy words which seems to carry several interpretations (Pring, 1973).[15] The common basic assumption is that barriers between subjects are to be broken down and links forged between hitherto separate parts of the curriculum. In terms of music education:

> The liberal education we all wish for our children implies a breadth of understanding and experience that will be possible only when we make conscious efforts to remove the boundaries between 'subjects'. (Paynter and Aston, 1970)[16]

The idea of 'removing boundaries', or 'breaking down barriers' between subjects is often given the status of automatically being a desirable state of affairs. Breaking down barriers is seen as a 'good' thing. The phrase is of course merely an analogy, a metaphor, and it is just as easily applied to have the reverse implications. For example, a leaking roof or a stomach ulcer is a broken barrier. A burst gasket on the engine of a car is a broken barrier often causing oil and water to mix in a disastrous way when the engine loses its integrity altogether. We should not assume, therefore, that the breaking down of barriers is always to be desired. We shall have to ask what then are the consequences and what we mean by breaking down barriers. Might it not sometimes be better to let things grow naturally and organically through and up the fences rather than to remove them altogether? Some clarification is required.

The root meaning of the word integration has to do with wholeness or soundness. It involves the idea of completion by adding necessary parts to make a whole or combining various elements into a new form. For music education in schools there seems to be two related yet different aspects which I will designate as *organization* and *stimulation*.

Organizationally there has been a tendency to group together certain subject areas under headings such as humanities, sciences, expressive arts. The reasons for this are not hard to find. Teachers of music, the visual arts movement and drama realize that they are stronger in the power structure of schools if they stand together and present a combined case for their subjects. The drama specialist is not always happy as a member of an English department which might emphasize literary skills instead of expressive art forms. Colleagues in Movement sometimes function uncomfortably as an annex to the P.E. department. The musician tends to be isolated from other colleagues by enormous lunch-time and after-school commitments. All realize that a case needs to be made for their areas of concern against the claims on time and resources put forward by the ostensibly more 'useful' subjects in the curriculum, science, maths, etc. We sense that the arts have the same fundamental functions in the lives of human beings, although they may operate in very different ways. We also need the active collaboration and participation of colleagues in combined ventures such as plays, operas and dance. In some schools, therefore, the organization of the time-table has been radically changed to permit team-teaching and the evolution of combined projects. In this there are great professional and social benefits. We are able to make a new start, to see what we do in a different way. The students can be hived off into different purposeful groups and staff can help one another in teaching rather than merely through staff-room conversations. However, it is clear that this kind of reorganization does not of itself produce integration in any real sense. A fairly common practice has been to settle for a 'topic' to which each

specialist can offer his or her particular contribution: 'The Sea', 'Our
Town', 'African Culture and its Effect on World Culture', are
examples. So one group will work on 'Sea' paintings, another on 'Sea'
music and a third on dance and movement tht exemplifies aspects of
wind and waves and so on. Ideally, the groups will meet from time to
time to work together, but often there is little interaction, except
perhaps in a public presentation of some kind. The crucial point is that
integration only takes place when one activity directly influences and
helps to shape the form of another. It is not enough merely to run
several activities together in the same organizational harness. They
must connect and interact, and this interaction takes place through the
conceptual and feeling processes of the participants.

This brings us to the second aspect, that of stimulation. True integration is not achieved organizationally but through the imagination
of particular people resulting in a special kind of product. When this
happens the effect can be very powerful indeed. In Bergman's well-
known film *Wild Strawberries* there is a moment when the central
character is in a procession to a university to receive an honorary
degree. For this and other reasons he is charged with a feeling of
elation. We hear the music of trumpets and the camera shows us the
moving foliage of trees through which a bright sun dazzles the eye.
The bright sound of trumpets integrates with the brilliance of the
sun's rays, the shape of these rays takes on at times almost the shape of
trumpet bells, and the quality of light is 'brassy'. All this echoes and
re-echoes the feeling experience of the character; indeed it *reveals* that
experience to us in a way that acting alone might never achieve. The
various elements are not merely combined but interact. The possibilities in one mode of experience trigger off, stimulate potential in
another. The imagination of the director is fired by a wealth of
imagery grouped around a concept – call it 'elation' perhaps or something else, a single word ceases to do it justice.

So it is with real integration in school. Take a concept, 'darkness',
for example. Make the darkest sounds to be found with the resources
available. Give the darkness form by growing and receding. Can this
form be taken up in movement? Can we write prose or poetry that,
superimposed or read separately, holds the same quality of
experience? Do these words give us any indication of what might
happen during, before or after this dark experience? How might we
best present the whole fusion to an audience who may not have been
involved with these processes so far? More than team-teaching or

time-table change is involved here. Indeed, a single teacher with imagination and the power to stimulate by suggestion or even silence may well have more effect than any pre-conceived and arbitrary 'topic'.

Once again we may note the exclusive nature of 'integration' if it were to be held as axiomatic for 'creativity', in that non-integrated activities would fall out of the 'creative' category. Theoretically this is unlikely, though in practice we ought to notice the strong connections and that 'most schools that have attempted to integrate music with other studies appear to have done so mainly for the opportunities provided for creativity' (Schools Council, 1972).

Before going further then, we could say that in music education the concept of creativity current in the 1970s implies the following conditions, at least in practice:

1. A premium on imaginative activities
2. An emphasis on children making up their own music
3. Sympathy with the techniques of the *avant garde*
4. An urge to integrate

Now there is much here that is of value and I am personally enthusiastic about many of the activities that flourish under the creativity movement. What is worrying is that it is an umbrella, a kind of progressive package-deal that carries with it a certain prestige. The word 'creative' does not merely apply as a term of description to particular types of activities in schools: it is value-laden, and is sometimes set up in contrast with the worst rather than the best of other activities: 'Through creative music it becomes possible for a majority of pupils of all ages and abilities to experience the deep satisfaction of participation' (Department of Education, 1970).

The objection still stands against the use of the term as an evaluation that implies the exclusion of other ways of engaging with children in musical activities. If neutral words like improvisation and composition were used instead, then I for one would be happier. As it stands we must press towards changes of conceptual attachment that will take in more than current usage implies. When third-year boys in a secondary school display the imagination required to improvise tunes in a well-assimilated 'blues' style over a collective chordal accompaniment, I cannot help but see it as 'creative', even though the style is not contemporary and the activity not 'integrated'. When a first-year group, with or without help from the teacher, manage to shape and phrase someone else's song with a feeling for the sense of the words and the melodic line, I feel obliged to regard it as an achievement of imagination and sensitivity, no matter that they did not make up the piece for themselves. Might they not be said to have 'created' the music? After all, it would be possible to find dismal and dull performances of the same song where no atmosphere or 'feeling' emerged, or, in other words, where nothing was 'created'. One is reminded that the composer Vaughan Williams once indicated to Sir Adrian Boult that he, the conductor, had actually 'created' the second movement of the Fourth Symphony, as the composer had not really known himself how it should be performed. One is also reminded that at times certain actors are said to have 'created' particular roles in the theatre.

It may be possible to widen the applicability of creativity even further if we are prepared to regard imagination as the keystone and waive the other three conditions. A composer's view of the 'gifted listener' is of interest here, and well describes the art of audition.

> Nothing really tells him what he should be hearing, no treatise or chart or guide can ever sufficiently pull together the various strands of a complex piece of music – only is inrushing floodlight of one's own imagination can do that. Recognising the beautiful in an abstract art like music partakes somewhat of a minor miracle; each time it happens I remain slightly incredulous. (Aaron Copland, 1952)[17]

Even 'mere' listening then cannot be conceived as a passive state. It requires a lively imagination, alert and sympathetic attention, a mind able to make a ('creative'?) leap into the thinking and feeling of other people. It also, at times, demands staying power.

In short, I would pick out the first clause in the creativity canon as being fundamental to the situation. Imagination is the unchanging variable. The other three are simply some ways of turning loose the images – valuable, but not inevitable.

We ought to notice one other thing about creativity. When the term is applied to achievements in maths, science and elsewhere, there are two conditions usually in evidence along with any crucial imaginative act. The first of these is a background of knowledge, skills and experience in the particular field of activity to which a particular problem is related. The second is that any 'creations' are verified, tested, either by rigorous reasoning and debate, or by controlled experiments, or, in the case of technology, by whether the thing works or not. Over those rarer moments of inspiration, the flashpoints of original ideas, we seem to have little control, and they may indeed 'arrive when least expected, perhaps uninvited, when relaxing rather than working: certainly they will rarely come to order, or in a contrived "let's be creative" session. But however and whenever they come, the ground is prepared beforehand and the novelty tested after its emergence.

"There are thousands of idle 'geniuses' who require to learn that, without a degree of industry in preparation and verification, no great intellectual work can be done . . ." (Wallas, 1970)[18]

Turning to the arts we are also made aware of a strong emphasis on work, struggle and skill that surrounds and makes possible 'creativity'. Zola tells us in his introduction to *L'Oeuvre* that 'I shall recount my own intimate life as a creative artist, the everlasting pains of childbirth'. Tchaikovsky indicates something of his processes in a letter dated 7 July 1778.

What has been set down in a moment of ardour must now be critically examined, improved, extended, or condensed, as the form requires. Sometimes one must do oneself violence, must sternly and mercilessly erase things thought out with love and enthusiasm.

Copland (1952) believes that music is particularly demanding among the arts.

Music boasts no Henri Rousseau, no Grandma Moses. Naiveté doesn't work in music. To write any sort of usable piece presumes a minimum kind of professionalism.

Now all this is very different from much 'creative' music in education. Here the emphasis tends to be on instant results, and any evaluation of the product is likely to be discouraged by drawing attention to the value of the activity for the participants. And there may be many situations in which this is appropriate. We need to remember, however, that there can be stimulation of the imagination through the ideas of other people, that the need to feel a sense of achievement and mastery is also a part of 'creative' behaviour, and that respect and admiration for a good product is a vital piece of the whole business.

So while we rightly value the imaginative processes involved, can we also ask for consideration of a wider field of experience than those associated with the 1970s concept of creativity? Amongst these would be imaginative activities without necessarily the production of an originally composed, or quasi *avant garde,* or instantly integrated artifact. We must also find a place for the development of skills that allow the imagination to range far afield, unlimited by scanty resources.

It is here that the idea of C(L)A(S)P comes into its own to promote fluency, flexibility (or divergence), originality, sensitivity to problems and the redefinition of the familiar. We should work freely across the model by playing roles relating to music; the roles of composer, performer, auditor, also having experience in the subordinate activities of literature studies and skill-learning. We then stand some chance of producing a state of affairs where pupils and ourselves are more free to make appropriate connections, to redefine music and to find those modes of relationship which are most productive for particular individuals. We shall certainly find that involvement with a broad range of musical styles is a consequence of this way of approaching our work.

I have tried to present the case that creativity is not the prerogative of composers. Performers and auditors also have the opportunity to create for themselves or others alternative worlds of experience through their relationship with and response to music. It is even possible to find the creativity thread running through literature studies and skill acquisition. After all, one can approach musical literature more or less imaginatively and gain insight into style and form that illuminate music in a new way. It is certainly risky to assume that skills are always assembled in a painstaking and 'convergent' way. Sometimes we suddenly get flashes of revelation as to how we might approach a technical problem, we see how it can be managed, we have imagined a solution, we have created a new cluster of technical possibilities. However, I would not wish to press this too far. The important thing is to be alive to the possibilities of creative behaviour across the spectrum of C(L)A(S)P activities, to work in a relevant way between the five areas and to use the model to span whichever of the available musics of today seem appropriate to the particular setting in which we find ourselves working.

References
1. ROGERS, C.R. (1954). 'Towards a Theory of Creativity'. In: Vernon, P.E. (Ed) *Creativity*. Penguin, 1970. 137-51.
2. STORR, A. (1972). *The Dynamics of Creation*. Pelican. 1976.
3. GUILFORD, J.P. (1959). 'Traits of Creativity'. In: Vernon, P.E. (Ed) *Creativity*. Penguin, 1970. 167-87.
4. BURT, C.L. (1962). 'Critical Notice: The Psychology of Creative Ability'. In: Vernon, P.E. (Ed) *Creativity*. Penguin, 1970. 203-16.
5. ELLIOTT, R.K. (1971). *Versions of Creativity*. Proceedings of the Philosophy of Education Society of Great Britain, Vol. V., No. 2, July 1971.

6. HUDSON, L. (1966). 'The Question of Creativity'. In: Vernon, P.E. (Ed) *Creativity*. Penguin, 1970. 217-34.

7. BERLIOZ, H., translated (1970). *The Memoirs of Hector Berlioz*. Panther. 578-9. CAIRNS, D.

8. WALLACH, M.A. and KOGAN, N. (1965). 'A New Look at the Creativity – Intelligence Distinction'. In: Vernon, P.E. (Ed) *Creativity*. Penguin, 1970. 235-56.

9. SINNOTT, E.W. (1959). 'The Creativeness of Life'. In: Vernon, P.E. (Ed) *Creativity*. Penguin, 1970. 107-15.

10. DEPARTMENT OF EDUCATION AND SCIENCE (1970). *Creative Music in Schools*.

11. SCHOOLS COUNCIL (1972). *Music and Integrated Studies in the Secondary School*.

12. SELF, G. (1967). *New Sounds in Class – A Contemporary Approach to Music*. Universal: London.

13. MANHATTANVILLE MUSIC CURRICULUM PROGRAM (1970. Media Materials, Inc. Bardonia, N.Y.

14. SMALL, C. (1977). *Music, Society, Education*. John Calder: London.

15. PRING, R. (1973). *Curriculum Integration: the need for clarification*. The New Era. (54,3).

16. PAYNTER, J. and ASTON, P. (1970). *Sound and Silence – Classroom Projects in Creative Music*. Cambridge.

17. COPLAND, A. (1952). *Music and Imagination*. Mentor Books.

18. WALLAS, G. (1926). 'The Art of Thought'. In: Vernon, P.E. (Ed) *Creativity*. Penguin, 1970. 91-7.

Chapter 6:

Music, Society and the Individual

We have so far been considering the central issue in music education, that of music as aesthetic experience. In Chapter 3 we noted the parameters of musical experience under the model of C(L)A(S)P and that there can be no short cuts to aesthetic experience via analysis and history of music or through sociology and ethnomusicology. However, we must notice now that music takes place in a social context and that there is bound to be an interaction between the making and response to musical objects and social attitudes and conditions.

Our musical experiences whether in the act of composition, audition or performance are undoubtedly influenced and to some extent shaped by four variables.

1. *Personality dispositions,* physiological and psychological;
2. *Specific musical ideas,* intrinsic to musical objects, the musical 'gestures' and stylistic relationships between norms and deviations;
3. *Available skills and technology,* especially the evolution of particular instruments and other sound sources;
4. *Social influences,* especially when music is an integral part of social events, or signifies that the participants belong to a particular group in society.

It is mainly the last of these that concerns us now, but first we ought to remind ourselves that the third area, the influence of skills and technology, is of some importance in determining both style and expressive gesture in music. In the first chapter, I gave one or two

examples of the influence of what I called musical *materials* on the
elements that emerge from them. We can understand this a little better
by projecting ourselves in imagination into the setting of what is
sometimes called 'primitive society'. Let us then in our 'minds eye'
watch a 'primitive' man at work (or is it at play?), carving away at a
piece of stick and singing as he whittles. Like the wood in his hands his
tune has shape, a satisfying structure in the making. The song takes a
life of its own, an individual, recognizable identity. It has become an
objective 'thing', like the object in his hands, which can be taken up,
left alone, altered or passed to someone else. Some early communities
speak of a tune being 'caught' like a ball or 'carried' by a group of
singers like a pot or a boat. We might notice that the hollow wooden
object nearing completion in our subject's hands is turning out to be a
simple form of pipe. He tests it and tunes it until it works well enough
to 'hold' tunes. The point here is that it is not very likely that any tunes
he plays will be similar to the tunes he sings. The feel of the instrument, its timbre and touch, the physical sensation of blowing and the
buzz of vibration at the finger ends will probably suggest musical
elements quite different from those evolving through the voice. Here
then is a sounding tool. Any resulting music is shaped to a certain
extent by what the tool is able to do, by the pipe as well as the piper. It
provides a definite framework of technical possibilities which is bound
to modify and even suggest intrinsically musical elements.

Specific examples of this are given by Professor John Blacking
(1976).[1] He makes some interesting observations concerning some
elements of tribal music in Zambia.

> Among the Nsenga of the Petauke district, boys play small
> *kalimba mbiras* as a diversion when they are sitting alone. Analysis
> of the tunes they play reveals relationships between the patterns
> of movement between the left and right thumb, the patterns of
> rhythm with which they pluck the 'keys', and the patterned
> arrangements of the 'keyboard' itself. The tunes do not sound like
> other Nsenga music . . . (p.12)

Here then we can see that the music is to some extent determined
by the instruments available and not exclusively by purely musical
ideas or traditions in any kind of abstract way. In our European
community we can see a similar pattern. The intensive and widespread
teaching of orchestral instruments leads to a situation where music is
to some extent defined in terms of how these instruments function,
especially in the context of the traditional classical orchestra. Amongst
many people there is then resistance to accepting as music sounds *not*

produced by such instruments. What 'counts as music' is partly determined by what counts as a musical instrument. We might also notice
at this point that music in school classrooms may often be seen by
pupils to be unrelated to music as they understand it outside of
school, precisely because the instruments used, often of the Orff
variety, do not feature very much in other forms of music outside.
Consequently the school may be seen to be operating a separate world
of music which may well seem unreal to many students. This sense of
unreality is further aggravated by social influences and especially by
the strong social bonds pupils may have formed through popular
music, compared with the weak reinforcement at home and amongst
peers for music as it is traditionally defined in many schools. We shall
therefore now consider the phenomenon of pop music since it is a very
clear example of social influences interacting with musical preferences
and involvement.

Nearly everything that is said about pop music is an over-
simplification in a complex area. A brief look at a few of the common
assumptions may help us to a sharper perspective.

1. *Pop music is 'the denegration of youth at the hands of the commercial
entertainers'* (David Holbrook). There are two main points at issue
here. It is of course obvious that pop music is a marketable product to
be bought and sold as any other product might be. It is also surrounded
by the inevitable paraphernalia of advertising and high-pressure sales
talk. This in itself however should not persuade us to dismiss out of
hand all music that appears under the pop 'label'. We ought to
recognize that commercial pressures and sales techniques are applied
to all kinds of music at all levels of our society. It is true that the modes
of advertisement and the social group influences relating to, say, opera
or the concert hall are more subtle than those flaunted by the media
with regard to pop, but that such pressures exist surely cannot be
denied. In any form of music we are aware that some performers are
seen to have 'star' quality which may fill a large hall, whatever the
musical programme. Reverence for, and adulation of a celebrated
performer is common across the whole spectrum of music. Once we
look beneath the surface, the presentation of particular musical items
is similar across the spectrum. Radio 1 may concern itself with the
positions of performers in the 'charts', thus giving some sense of shape
to the output and also indicating that what is being transmitted is
desirable and valued. Similarly, Radio 3 may be presenting 'this
week's composer', which again gives an arbitrary sense of structure to

the output and places a value on particular music and musicians. In the realm of advertising there are other equivalences. Every aspiring performer provides biographical information giving descriptions of his/her successes, life-style, musical background, experience. This is the same whether the market is classical, at music clubs and lunch-time concerts, or pop on the college campus and in civic halls. Any-one concerned with attracting an audience or the selling of records and tapes is bound to be promoting the product as effectively as possible. We cannot even say that so-called classical music is promoted solely on the basis of the intrinsic value within the music itself. Some advertisements quite shamelessly suggest that we might become members of a particular social group with a certain prestige and that the membership of such a group can be through purchase of particular musical items. For example, a set of records containing music from the Baroque era have been advertised on the grounds that these records will enable people to reach a 'depth of enjoyment that many people never find'. This is clearly an invitation to join a kind of club, to belong to a special social group.

The second point of issue here is whether we can ever say that music is the 'denegration' of any group of people. Certainly to assume that it is always the case with pop music is to be blind to the different ways in which we can respond to it. There are vast numbers of people coming into daily contact with pop music who will never find themselves in newspaper headlines describing scenes of violence or depravity and whose lives are not impoverished as a result.

2. *Children do/do not want popular music as part of the school curriculum.* One or other of these alternatives is usually taken up in discussions of this kind. In fact *four* clear clusters of attitudes have been isolated by Murdock and Phelps (1974)[2] in their survey concern-ing teachers and pupils. Briefly these run as follows:

popular music should be part of the school programme because it can be worthwhile;

popular music should be part of the school programme to show by comparison with other music how poor it is;

popular music should not be part of the school programme because it is essentially worthless;

popular music should not be part of the school programme, not because it is without value but because it has no place in school.

The general question as to whether or not pupils want to see pop in school divides them more or less equally between the answers yes and no. This is a point that must be noticed by those who advocate the inclusion of pop in the music curriculum as well as those who reject it.

3. *Pop music is only for adolescents.* This is obviously untrue, as even the most casual observation will reveal. The audience for radio programmes containing large amounts of pop music includes many adults who, for one reason or another, are at home or listening at work. Even the idea of 'adolescence' itself needs refining. We can distinguish more than one stage in the process of growing up. Even in the most general terms we might identify three main phrases, not one. They could be called pubescence, (nine to twelve years approximately) early adolescence (the characteristic third year group in secondary schools) and late adolescence (fifteen plus). These age groups are widely divergent in attitudes to school, to other people and to music. In secondary schools first year pupils are very different from those in the middle of the school, and different again are those young adults in the two or three years before leaving school at eighteen. We cannot assume that involvement with pop music, where it exists, will be of the same quality and intensity across these years of rapid change and growth.

4. *All pop music sounds the same.* Pop music may indeed sound the same to the uninitiated just as Mozart does, but to those who understand it and respond to it there are many differences in style and context. A closer examination of an average day of transmission on radio or of records on sale will reveal many different styles including possibly, reggae, soul, rock, progressive rock, folk music both rural and urban and songs with sensitive lyrics by 'intellectual' performers. There may also be sentimental or comic songs by professional entertainers and, now and then, some jazz or rag-time. We may hear a hymn tune played on bagpipes or an older song, once enjoyed by our grandparents, played on a brass band. Nor should we think that the 'charts' represent the full range of pop and allied music. West Indian communities in our large cities know reggae items that rarely, if ever, get a hearing on the radio. Progressive rock enthusiasts complain that their music is not adequately represented on the media. There is then a multiplicity of pop music rather than one style and it is certainly not accepted passively by all young adults. They are discriminating and choosing, selecting and rejecting, and those whose business it is to sell this music are well aware of differences in preference.

5. *Pop music is used in a different way from other forms of music.* The following quotation from Witkin (1974)[3] amplifies this view.

The music teacher seeks quite different things from the music than the pupil and the more he discusses the musical merits of pop the more he is asking the pupil to put music to quite a different use and one that is antithetical to the immediate gratification that it affords him. Pop music is not independent of the situation, moods, private and public places, and encounters that characterize adolescent life. Pop music is important to the adolescent in as much as it is expressive of part of his cultural milieu and of his consciousness within it. Since in much of school life and certainly in the music lesson the adolescent finds the expression of that consciousness denied, pop music played in schools for appreciation can seem like an empty gesture. (p.131)

This kind of judgment is based on an observation that pop music is *always* used as a kind of signal identifying social group giving status to those who subscribe to it and unifying people in a common concern. It is certainly true that popular music is often used in this way, but a deeper understanding and more sustained observation of children in their encounters with pop music will reveal that, for many, the music also functions in a *symbolic* way, expressive of feeling qualities and containing the structural elements of norm and deviation. Compare, for example, these two comments on the same song by two boys in the same third year class at school: 'This is the only group that can really sing'; and 'The second song is a kind of noisy sound and I could listen to it for ever. There is a ringing sound in it which I seem to wait for'. Here, in this second example, is a statement that appears to reveal a true aesthetic appreciation. This boy seems conscious not only of the gestures, the thrusting, 'noisy sound' of the music, but also of something which he waits for, a developed sense of expectation, a feeling for the structure of the piece. Of course, in a disco or in other public places pop music has a certain function which is undeniably social but even on these occasions it is possible to observe that every now and then there is greater attention to the intrinsic quality of the music. At such times social activity is subordinate to individual responses and a feeling within the group that each person is responding privately but powerfully. But the observation of the use of pop in public places will tell us very little compared with the way in which it is used by private individuals at home. There they may repeat a particular song many times, learning it, performing it with the recording, reading the words, relating to it. At such times pop is treated like any aesthetic object, an object that speaks, communicates a sense of presence, gives a sense of feelingfulness. I once overheard a boy in school comment to a friend during a class rehearsal of a ballad type of pop song, 'Every time I hear this song, I want to cry'. Many music lovers know this feeling.

To wear popular music as a badge, to fly it as a flag or to chant it as a kind of slogan is one thing, but there is this further element which has about it the characteristics of an aesthetic encounter. This is the area of our concern in music education. We know from research that popular music in school need not be an empty gesture provided that it is handled musically, sensitively and with sincerity (Sarah, 1974)[4]. Several positive approaches have been attempted, especially by Swanwick (1968 and 1975)[5], Spencer (1976)[6], and Burnett (1977)[7].

In the final analysis though, pop should find its way into school and college music courses only because as music it seems worthwhile. We are required as teachers to develop ourselves an understanding, responsive and discriminating attitude to pop music. This is particularly rewarding when the social environment of any school is such that some form of pop is the basic tradition which most students have assimilated. In this situation we build on what they already have; an ear for syncopation and swung rhythm; a knack with vocal melisma; a personal identification with the feelings that are presented in the music and the words. In some settings we may find that we cannot go very far beyond what the local background proscribes. The pipe-dream of more sophisticated rock musicians, that their world of music may be opened up for more people, might be as unthinkable as the vision that, somehow, attention to pop will lead to love of Beethoven. This is not the point of it. All is not lost if an awareness of the power of music to speak to us can be extended just a little and if the use of music as a cultural slogan and a divisive piece of social flag-waving can be fractionally reduced.

Pop music is an important phenomenon for music educators in that it embodies one of the central problems in education. It is one of the points where we key into the larger and more general debate about the nature of education, the relationship of school to society, the development of individuals and their role in a community. It also raises the difficult question of what are sometimes called 'standards', in education. The issues may become clearer if we consider three main positions frequently taken by music educators.

1. *Music is part of our cultural heritage.* Pop music can thus be seen as either a betrayal of this heritage at the hands of commercial exploiters or as a legitimate part of such a heritage following on from the older folk tradition.

2. *Music is socially determined.* On this view pop music is a legitimate form of music arising from a particular social setting. All the arts are a series of mirrors reflecting the conditions under which they come about. The only question of value therefore, is whether or not a particular art object truly reflects its social setting.

3. *Music is for personal development.* On this view the emphasis is not so much on cultural relics of the past or even on present day cultural manifestations but on the power of music to somehow influence and develop human feelings. Whether or not pop music is able to do this will depend on its use, whether as a sign of social status or a symbol of human feeling.

Each of these positions brings its own particular light to music education along with its own special obscurities and dangers. Let us briefly consider each in turn and in doing so, widen the scope of our discussion.

1. *Music is part of our cultural heritage.* It is this view which forms what is sometimes called the 'traditional' approach to music education. Important here is the transmission of knowledge and skills from one generation to another. Music becomes part of what is called a liberal education. To be educated then means in part to be an *inheritor,* someone who has taken over the best things from the past thus gaining a perspective on the present and the possibility of projecting a future. Schools and teachers are therefore rather like a set of filters, selecting and preserving that information, understanding and skill which seems to be of most value. The act of selection does of course include rejection and this view of education has built into it a value system which strains out those things considered to be not worthwhile. In the case of music the emphasis is obvious. There will be a commitment to the passing on of traditional skills, especially in instrumental playing and composing. Ability with a musical instrument is a kind of key, especially to the past. It allows us to unlock doors marked Beethoven, Bach, Byrd, and so on. Along with instrumental skill runs the ability to read music, especially traditional notation which is yet another key unlocking doors to the culture of the past. Connected with this would be an emphasis on a historical perspective of music, the sound and function of musical instruments at different times, the development of musical forms and the acquisition of aural discrimination. Practical implications for teachers involved a high degree of structure; for example, consider the hundreds of instructional 'tutors' for piano or for violin. Methods may vary but each course tends to be systematic, carefully

built in graded stages. The same is also true for the Kodaly Choral Method, with its many exercises and tunes for every stage of development. One consequence of such a structured approach is that it becomes fairly easy to specify clear objectives and also to evaluate the progress of students. We can think of the Associated Board examinations, of GCE and CSE in music, and of the multiplicity of degrees or degree-units involving music in our universities or colleges.

Critics of this view rightly point out that the music of the past was once the music of the *present* and, as such, directly influenced people living at the time. We saw in Chapter 5 that it is unhelpful to consider as contemporary music *only* the music that is *composed* today, but better to view it as music which is *available* today. However, this does not absolve us from involving ourselves and our students in aspects of contemporary music in the limited sense or from noticing that some music under the pop label may well be an important contemporary manifestation of the arts. The greatest difficulty of the traditional view hinges on the concept of relevance. If we define music in such narrow terms as part of our 'cultural heritage' then it will cease to have relevance for many people in our multi-cultural society. Worse than this, it is possible to venerate skills and techniques along with historical study as though these were the crucial and central parts of music experience. There is however value in certain aspects of the traditional view. In particular it is strongly achievement-centred, which is psychologically powerfully motivating for those who succeed in the skills and knowledge required. It also really does preserve for us strong musical objects from the past that may still speak to us directly and inform our contemporary experience. The view then is not without virtue, though taken alone it can be very limiting.

2. *Music is socially determined.* The desire to see music as being almost entirely socially determined is an echo of a larger debate at the roots of educational, and especially sociological theory. Basically, the 'new' sociology runs along these lines: different human cultural groups and sub-cultures regard and value knowledge in different ways; knowledge is therefore 'problematic' in that it is impossible to specify what is worthwhile and desirable in any universal sense, least of all for a society that is mixed in ethnic origins and divided over what it regards as valuable and necessary. Accordingly, the ways in which teachers and others select a range of knowledge and skills to be transmitted as part of a 'cultural heritage' are open to question. It may be that teachers ought not to categorize the cultural background of

pupils as in some way inferior, or in deficit, but merely as *different*. These problems are raised by various contributors to *Knowledge and Control* (Young, 1971).[8] On this view we must seriously consider becoming bi-cultural as teachers, more like the people we teach, so that instead of seeking to change and educate in ways prescribed by 'middle-class' culture, we would be more concerned to strengthen the particular sub-culture of students by entering it ourselves and building our curriculum from it to some extent. The implication for those in music education is clear:

> . . . the music of the masters was never intended for the broad mass of people who were non-receptive to the heritage of the past and who in every age have had their own more direct and exuberant folk and dance music. Our teaching is not confined to the successors of the 'folk' as well. It is a fallacy to assume that universal acceptance of the cultural heritage of the 17th, 18th and 19th centuries. (ILEA, 1973)[9]

We might add to this that the more complex and involved forms of music produced by contemporary composers in the twentieth century are similarly restricted to the successors of this cultural élite.

We do not have to look very far for our 'folk' music today. It is undoubtedly located mainly in the pop music system, reaching vast numbers of people, especially those of school age. In a plea for us to consider Afro-American music on its own cultural terms Graham Vulliamy makes the following point 'Academic music in this country is totally dominated by music in the European serious tradition: neither 'O' or 'A' level consider Afro-American music at all in any of its forms . . . (1976).[10]

The parameters of the 'new' sociology and the implications for education have been well examined by Lawton (1975)[11]. They are, that the present structure of education in our society preserves the *status quo* in an unjust way. Knowledge is socially distributed and some people are more powerful than others in the way they have access to and are able to manipulate knowledge. Knowledge is therefore stratified in our society, and subject barriers, which are artificial and arbitrary, are used to determine and define knowledge. This view suggests that all knowledge is thus socially constructed and is therefore relative in value. Lawton makes the point here that teachers would certainly benefit from this kind of examination of aspects of their teaching style and pupil relationships, and indeed from a redefinition of what 'counts as knowledge' in the school curriculum.

But he also points out that if all knowledge is of equal value then why do we have schools at all? And most of all 'if rationality is relative is there any point in talking to each other, let alone writing books?'

The main difficulty for teachers would seem to be in precisely this last comment, namely that we are unable to structure education at all if we regard all activities as of equal worth and refuse to attempt to predict outcomes of teaching and learning in the form of a curriculum, or even a specific set of objectives for a single session. This is indeed one of the significant problems of a social and relativistic view of knowledge, though as a comment about the inflexibility and rigidity of much curriculum planning and many teaching strategies it has validity. It is well expressed by Christopher Small in *Music – Society – Education* (1977)[12].

> The outward and visible sign of the subject is the syllabus, a table of contents that lays down what the student is required to learn and on what he is to be examined. At least, that is what the syllabus purports to do; in practice it equally effectively cuts him off from learning, since everything lying outside the syllabus is not examinable and therefore not worth teaching. The syllabus narrows the student's vision of knowledge and cuts him off from precisely those fuzzy areas at the edges of subjects that are the most interesting and rewarding . . . (p.186)

We should notice though, that we do not need to equate a syllabus with examinations, nor do we need to restrict possible learning outcomes to those we attempt to predict, but a teacher in order to be truly professional must engage students in what he considers to be worthwhile activities, and therefore is obliged to think out grounds for these and to express them in some form of statement, or at least bear them in mind as the enterprise proceeds. This does demand a constant re-thinking, re-evaluation, re-perception of pupils and subject, in short, awareness and flexibility. If a curriculum is stated, in other words if it becomes a syllabus, it is at least then honest and open. It can be challenged or changed, departed from, shared, discussed, used in public debate. It will enter into the very fabric of the processes of our continually changing view of teaching and learning. Small himself has performed a very stimulating service in clarifying and revealing some of the often forgotten issues underlying music education and there are consequences in what he says that will bear upon the practice of teaching and our total approach to music as a human activity in society.

The point at issue here tends to revolve around the dichotomy between *process and products*. The idea of process emphasizes the never-ending evolution of each human personality which is not susceptible to evaluation, examination or highly structured teaching. Concern with products on the other hand is an emphasis on what people actually produce, the objects they make, the things they say. This debate takes many forms and the idea of a specified curriculum clearly indicates a valuing of products rather than a reverence for individual processes. Various polarities in the debate tend to give different slants to the argument. We can set the idea of educational standards against individual development; the basic idea of a 'core' curriculum versus personal choice; telling people versus discovery; informing versus exploration; public performance versus private development. However, we ought to notice that this apparent distinction is really quite false. At any stage of a personal process a product exists, even if it is only a half formulated idea, a group composition in the making, or whatever. Processes essentially take place *on* products, not in the abstract. We have to be thinking about *something*, imagining *something*, making *something*. This is not an abstract activity without any visible signs. Nor can we assume that we can somehow directly influence people's processes. We can only relate to other people through their products, what they say and do. Essentially private processes are publicly manifested through the products, which may be regarded as provisional, but are always important from the point of view of human communication. Without products we have nothing we can say to one another and no means of saying it. There is, in short, nothing to talk about or to do. We might also notice that one person's product becomes part of another's processes. What is said or done by someone is bound to have some influence on the thinking and feeling of someone else. This is obviously true of art works, which while being products are still the result of personal processes and do impinge directly and powerfully on the processes of those who engage with them. Because products are the public, essential means of sharing experience we gain feedback and reinforcement which stimulates and motivates us. This is crucial for further development.

It is at this point that we notice that we are inevitably assessing or evaluating products as they come before us. This does not mean that we are necessarily enmeshed in a scheme of formal examinations, or being critical in some way. Life depends on assessing and evaluating what is happening; we estimate, judge, gauge, weigh up situations. For example, riding a bicycle is a *process,* but falling off or staying on the bicycle is a *product* by which the process is assessed. So let us not assume that somehow we can deal with abstract processes without regard to products. We can only meet each other in products. They are all we can handle. They are the only ways in which human beings can connect with one another.

If we do so venerate personal processes that we become reluctant to formulate any kind of curriculum or specify manageable objectives we shall eventually be driven to abandon the idea of education altogether, or at least to try to establish a totally different role for schools. The argument will then run as follows: all knowledge is provisional and is relative between social groups; within social groups individual development is of paramount importance; schools as they exist at present tend to operate to rigid curricula reinforced by examinations; this is totally against the concept of reinforcing particular sub-cultures and against idea of the freedom of individual development; therefore, we ought to abandon the idea of formal schooling or at least modify it in the direction of much greater flexibility. We would move towards what John Holt calls schools with a small 's' (1976)[13].

No doubt our schools have been partly responsible for producing an attitude of mind that looks upon education as a way of acquiring value-tickets, passports to security, wealth and power but this does not necessarily lead us to abandon the concept of schooling altogether nor to reject any idea of structuring education in some form or other. The view of Small and others draws on experience with communities outside of the western tradition to show the relative richness of different social structures where there is little or no formal schooling. Against this we ought to set the carefully argued evidence of Bruner, gathered from similar societies.

> Less demanding societies – less demanding intellectually – do not produce as much symbolic embedding and elaboration of first ways of looking and thinking. Whether one wishes to 'judge' these differences on some universal human scale as favouring an intellectually more evolved man is a matter of ones values but however one judges, let it be clear that a decision not to aid the intellectual maturation of those who live in less technically developed societies cannot be premissed on the careless claim that it makes little difference. (Bruner, 1972, p.67)[14]

Also, from the same text, we might notice Bruner's caution on the problems of merely reinforcing a local culture, no matter how rich or intensely personalized.

> Very early too they learn in-group talk and thinking and, just as their language use reflects less long-range goal analysis, it tends towards a parochialism that makes it increasingly difficult to move or work outside the poverty neighbourhood and the group. (p.179)

In other words we need to balance our concern for different cultural values against the need to create opportunities and flexibility within a larger and changing community. This is not an easy road to tread and is fraught with problems which account for the interminable debates on this issue and for the difficulties teachers face, especially in urban schools, of selecting materials and objectives which take into account both the local culture and the wider culture beyond the geographical area or the confines of poverty. For music education this does indeed mean that teachers must, in a sense, become bi-cultural, able to sympathize with and work in areas of music familiar to students but also able to identify the important musical concepts and understanding and skills that enable people to reach out, when they feel they might, to extend and refine their handling of musical elements.

Before leaving the issue of social relevance we ought to consider an extreme case where music is seen to be almost entirely socially determined. I refer especially to the work of John Shepherd in *Who's Music?* (1977)[15]. Shepherd attempts to show that particular materials of music evolved as 'part of the ongoing construction of social reality'. He claims that 'the organization of musical structures is ultimately a dialectic correlate of the social reality that is symbolically mediated by and through the music of a particular society' (p.84). He gives two particular instances which he works out in some detail. In one of these he argues that 'the pentatonic structure underlying much mediaeval music in itself serves to articulate the ideal feudal structure'. This is based on the view that though any note in a pentatonic structure may be stressed more than the others, pentatonic tones are mutually dependent on one another and immediate in relationships, as are people in mediaeval society. There is no hierarchical structure, as in the tonal system, which Shepherd sees as 'encoding' the industrial world sense.

> In this fashion the architectonisism of the tonal structure articulates the world sense of industrial man, for it is a structure

having one central viewpoint (that of the key note) that is the focus of the single, unified sound-sense involving a high degree of distancing. (p.105)

This, for Shepherd, is a reflection of a hierarchical society where state, church, and aristocracy form the upper reaches and others take lower places in a fixed and large-scale system.

Unfortunately, this view concerns itself exclusively with musical *materials*, that is to say, with sound structures. These may indeed be limited by and dependent on certain social factors. But we have also seen that they owe something to the development of instruments which depends to a large extent on what is physiologically possible and also on the kind of raw materials to hand. Even if we take into account all these influences we are still left with the irreducable fact that musical *elements* themselves generate and extend ideas as they interact with one another in the imagination of composer or performer. Whatever the social system, we can find examples of musicians working within the same constraints of available resources and in the tradition of a particular style but producing musical objects vastly different from each other. We cannot say that classical symphonies are merely a 'coding' of the same ideology just because they all work to the tonal system and display surface similarities in musical form and style. It is what happens *inside* a given framework that counts; the deviations from the norms, the particular personal gestures of a composer. It is these things to which we are able to relate across historical time and cultural differences, and it is this which accounts for the fact that we can be responsive to music that is from a quite alien social structure, provided that we are prepared to accept the prevailing musical norms. So on the one hand we can note with Blacking, that

> The principles of musical organization must be related to social experiences, of which listening to and performing music form one aspect. The minuet is not simply a musical form borrowed from dancing: it has entirely different social and emotional associations before and after the French Revolution.

But also we must note with Blacking,

> Music can transcend time and culture. Music that was exciting to the contemporaries of Mozart and Beethoven is still exciting, although we do not share their culture and society. The early Beatles songs are still exciting although the Beatles have unfortunately broken up. Similarly some Venda songs that must have been composed hundreds of years ago still excite the Venda,

and they also excite me . . . I am convinced that the explanation for this is to be found in the fact that at the level of deep structures in music there are elements that are common to the human psyche, although they may not appear in the surface structures. (p.108)

It is precisely these *deep structures* that we have been concerned with in the earlier chapters and it is the deep structures that we shall seek out in music education, the sense of velocity, of movement, of pause, of tension, of resolution, growth and decay, a feeling of weight, space and size, and above all the recognition of a musical object as a presence impinging upon us and into which we must enter responsively.

3. *Music is for personal development.* In conclusion I should like to return once again to what I regard as the central area of our concern, to the relationship of individual with art object. In particular I wish to refer to the work of Witkin and Ross (1974, 1975, 1978). I shall not attempt to summarize the complexities of their arguments but to isolate what seems to me to be the crucial point at issue. 'It is our view that the prime concern of the arts curriculum should be with the emotional development of the child through creative self expression.' (Ross, 1975)[16].

There is an emphasis in both writers on this aspect which seems to centre on a view that we experience feelings in a fairly chaotic way and that through artistic creation this chaos can be ordered, the problems defined and externalized. Ross puts it like this:

When we have aroused, or sensed within us, an expressive feeling seeking form we have a sensate difficulty. Before we can actually engage in subject-reflexive action we need to formulate this sensate difficulty as an expressive problem: that is to say, we need to grasp the sensate elements or material that complies the difficulty, and adopt one of the principles listed above as the means of imaging and resolving the difficulty. (Ross, 1978, p.98)[17]

There seems to be an emphasis here on artistic activity, and especially the creation of art objects, as a chrystallization of personal feeling problems. Both Witkin and Ross are aware that things are not as simple as this but I would like to emphasize one point. Relationships with art objects, whether making or receiving them, are not simply a question of resolving feeling difficulties. We do in fact have other ways of handling these problems; in social and interpersonal activities, in sleep and in dreaming. The arts seem to be important not so much in terms of the direct expression of feeling, with all the difficulties we have previously observed to attend this view, but in a more subtle way. Richard Wollheim (1968) puts it thus:

> Originally it was claimed that works of art were expressive of a certain state if and only if they had been produced in, and were capable of arousing to, that state. Now this claim has been dropped, and the link that is postulated between, on the one hand, the work and, on the other hand, the psychic state of either artist or spectator holds only via a supposition: 'if I were in that state . . .', 'if I were in other circumstances . . .' (p.44)[18]

What we are saying then is that in making or responding to an art object we are in a relationship that has about it a touch of make-believe; it might be so; what would happen if? How would it feel if we try it this way or that? In other words, experience of music as an art helps us to *explore* feelings rather than merely encapsulate them. The meaningfulness and feelingfulness of aesthetic experience is bound up with an exploding universe of possibilities, not with an implosive attention to our own feeling states. If this is what is meant by 'the emotional development of the child' then all is well.

We can now see that music and the arts take their place in human life as a powerful means of adaptation and evolution. In a sense they are concerned with the *space between* the individual and the community, between tradition and innovation, between biological replication and evolutionary development. They are events standing between our awareness of ourselves and our consciousness of every-thing which is *not* ourselves. The relationship is two-way. Music structures feeling but also impregnates structure with feeling. It is a merging of subjectivity and objectivity. The crucial concept here is not creative self-expression, or social relevance, or technical skill, it is *responsiveness*. To respond means to make an answer to, to show sensitiveness to and to correspond with. The ability to respond adequately to another person, an object, a life experience or whatever is a fundamental and crucial human attribute. To feel a lack of responsiveness is to go hungry, to find the world grey and bleak. It is to be depressed, starved of richness. Music and the arts are concerned with pure responsiveness contemplated and rejoiced in, delighted in and consciously sought. An aesthetic experience is primarily and always an intensified response raised into full consciousness. Aesthetic means to feel more powerfully, to perceive more clearly. Its oppsite is *anaesthetic*.

We might now summarize the discussion I have attempted during this book.

1. Music has 'meaning' which may be influenced by social settings but, at a profound level, operates through the biological and psychological characteristics of human beings.

2. This meaningfulness depends on a cognitive grasp of the relationship of norms and deviations within a particular style or work. We recognize within that context the gestures and postures, the ebbing and flowing of human experience.

3. On a second level of meaning, music has the power to change and influence our perspective on living, the way we see ourselves, the way we *feel* life. This level cannot be taught for but is always looked for.

4. In education we are seeking to bring about purposeful activities in the three main areas of composition, audition and performance, noticing that these are informed and reinforced by literature studies and skill acquisition.

5. Through activities in the parameters of C(L)A(S)P we are looking for the development in our students of the ability to locate norms across a wide range of musics and to engage on the first level of meaning, through the recognition and production of expressive gesture.

6. In order to bring this about we need to specify clear objectives, honestly acknowledging that we are seeking change and development in particular directions for our students.

7. Whilst we recognize social pressures and other forces at work influencing the development of music and individual response to it, we look to music to break the confines and constrictions of social group and class. Music is not only a mirror of its time and place but also a world of windows opening up many possibilities and alternatives.

For too long we have proceeded by trial and error, perhaps with the emphasis on error. In the context of 'education for everyone', and of large schools and complex social problems we badly need to find a perspective that does not constrict but does guide our thinking and inform our feeling and intuition. I offer this book in the hope that it moves in that direction.

*Whether society has felt music valuable or needful
I have gone on writing because I must. And I know
that my true function within a society which
embraces all of us, is to continue an age-old
tradition, fundamental to our civilization, which
goes back into pre-history and will go forward
into the unknown future. This tradition is to create
images from the depths of the imagination and to give
them form whether visual, intellectual or musical.
For it is only through images that the inner world
communicates at all. Images of the past, shapes of
the future. Images of vigour for a decadent period,
images of calm for one too violent. Images of
reconciliation for worlds torn by division. And
in an age of mediocrity and shattered dreams, images
of abounding, generous, exuberant beauty.*

MICHAEL TIPPETT (1974)
Moving Into Aquarius

Postscript:

Extract from the Diary of a Teacher

What follows is part of an article from *Music in Education* November 1978. In this article I give a very personal response to a fortnight spent in Brazil, teaching on the Seventh Contemporary Music Course in Latin America. I include it here because it seems to summarize the spirit behind the rest of this book and also shows that teaching is never 'safe'. There is always a degree of risk, uncertainty, and consequently there is always an element of discovery, no matter how experienced we may be.

We pick up the diary on Friday 13 January 1978, where I describe my second attempt to work with a large group of South American students, equally split between Spanish and Portuguese speakers and representing a wide range of age and musical experience.

Friday, 13 January. The teaching session was a disaster. To begin with I had chosen to 'use' a contemporary type of score using hands and voices. (There was no other equipment except a rough old piano.) As I had often suspected, this reduced the group to a set of automatons, 'barking at print' in the same way that traditional notation sometimes does. 'What are your objectives?' I was asked through the interpreter. I took this to mean 'Why the hell are you doing this?' Secondly, I gave an example of improvising music to words using an English text, intending to distribute a Portuguese poem (one set by Villa-Lobos) for the group to work with. Unfortunately time ran out on this and they were left with the impression that I had retreated into the English language in self-defence. Indeed, this could easily have been the case, for I was spending most of the day without the company of any

English-speaking person and the nearest I came to conversation over several hours was in execrable French with a singer of Arabic love-songs from Morocco. Thirdly, I was considerably embarrassed by the presence (as interpreter) of Violeta, an excellent teacher in her own right who knew the group quite well, was from South America, had been on the Course before and was working as an alternate lecturer.

I should explain that one quickly becomes aware of the reaction of South Americans. If they like what happens they smile, talk excitedly amongst themselves and embrace each other and the teacher/lecturer at the end of sessions. If things do not go so well they want to know why. Accordingly, two Argentinian ladies came afterwards and inter-rogated me through the interpreter. Why do you not relate to us? Were you satisfied with the session? Why don't you relax more? Are you tired after travelling? No, I explained, I was not happy with the session, and especially with the three languages problem. In fact I was by now bleakly depressed. I felt like a student on teaching practice. I had misread the culture of the group. I had failed to relate properly. I had 'used' an activity which I did not value, and worse, all this in front of a kind of 'tutor'.

The final indignity on this black Friday, the 13th, was a Course staff meeting called to find out what travel arrangements needed to be made for return journeys. The discussion settled down into French rather than Spanish or Portuguese, it being assumed that the Germans and Belgian present would understand and that I could manage it. Imagine waiting your turn to be asked in a room full of people intent on your answers, in French: On what day do you leave? At what time? How much will it cost? What arrangements have been made so far? What would you like us to do for you? I did the best I could and slunk off. I was a dismal failure.

That night it poured with rain and as I watched the floods rising over the road I once again became a student teacher. 'If it rains any more the roads will be impassable and I shall not be able to get into the town tomorrow to take the class. Please let it rain some more!' I spent the rest of the night preparing and re-thinking the problem until, as D.H. Lawrence once sensitively observed, 'the mark was burned in and the pain burned out'.

Saturday, 14 January the floods had subsided. We agreed that the group should be split into Spanish/Portuguese speakers and that Violeta would take turns with them and not interpret. This was to be done by the person I was staying with and by the one English speaker in the student group. Because of these arrangements I was off the hook until Monday, but I made desperate efforts to communicate with every person I met. If I couldn't talk to them at least I could grin and shake hands and pass the salt at the table.

Sunday, 15 January The floods from the mountains had reached Sao Joao and people were cheerfully mopping out the houses near the river.

Monday, 16 January The class went well. In a workshop style of teaching I dealt with the irregular rhythmic metres which were part of the common musical heritage of the group, and with syncopation and jazz which are not so common in the forms we know in Latin America. We worked for a while on the Portuguese poem and then, in two separate groups, prepared a free composition with the poem as its basis. At the end I was (literally) patted on the back.

Tuesday, 17 January They brought along an improvised Samba using matchboxes, as promised yesterday, and I instigated a blues improvisastion. By now I was really liking these people with their warmth, vitality and quick responses. They sang with great verve. I was also enjoying the music itself, not just using it, and I moved away from merely *avant garde* idioms and instead crossed and re-crossed the boundaries of different musical styles.

Before going to bed I prepared myself for the Spanish-speaking group the next day. I found a poem by Antonio Machado which seemed to me to sound very beautifully and present striking images. 'The students might find it difficult' warned my translator/host. 'Never mind, what does it all mean?'

Wednesday, 18 January With fingers crossed I have the poem intoned until it begins to take musical shape. After a while we are completely immersed in the images and sonorities of the words and music. At the end of the class one of my lady critics from Friday comes up and trembles her hand over her head to represent electricity between us and around us: and this without any common language at all. I mime my thanks and shrug off the implications.

At this point I had rediscovered some of the fundamentals of teaching. They reduce to four simple principles.

1. *Always relate to people.* Occupying them is not enough.
2. *Find out what you can about the culture* in which you find yourself and signal your willingness to participate in it. Then go beyond it.
3. It is a necessary (though not by itself sufficient) condition that *teachers must themselves be excited* to some degree by the activity in process at any given time.

4. *Go for the deep structure of the subject.*

In music this means getting to grips with its materials, its forms and its sense of impact, or expressiveness, across different styles. This may be a rather difficult point which might become clearer if I relate it to the culture and language problem I had experienced. One becomes more conscious of having a culture when one steps outside it. We become more aware of the structure, inflections and shades of meaning in language when we are confronted with other languages. Our sense of how a language and a culture works is built up in part from many experiences across different cultures and languages. In music education the same seems to apply. We become more sensitive to the central concepts of pitch and rhythm variation, of timbre and texture change, by seeing them at work over a range of styles and periods. We learn to adjust our perceptions to a level appropriate to a particular idiom. In a strange way it seems that the necessity to adjust to the grosser differences as, say, between Handel and Boulez may help to sensitize us to the more subtle differences of dialect and personal manner, for example, as between Haydn and Mozart. We also become aware that people do speak sincerely with different musical voices and consequently are less embarrassed, more tolerant, as we, so to speak, travel abroad musically, meeting other styles than those close to hand.

As a corollary to this we might also look for flexibility in the roles we play relating to music. We can be composers (including improvisors); auditors (aesthetically responsive listeners); or performers (at any level of accomplishment). We might at times find ourselves engaging in the activities of skill acquisition (getting something technically right, aural development, using notation); or literature studies (the literature of music and the literature about music, history, analysis, etc.). By approaching music in these various ways we multiply the chances that we, and our students, will perceive music more acutely and respond more profoundly.

The crucial thing, though, is not to confuse flexibility with floppiness. The only thing that matters ultimately is the sense of commitment to the activity of the *here and now, the integrity of the particular experience.*

References
1. BLACKING, J. (1976). *How Musical is Man?* Faber.
2. MURDOCK, G. and PHELPS, G. (1973). *Mass Media and the Secondary School.* Schools Council.

3. WITKIN, R.W. (1974). *The Intelligence of Feeling.* Heinemann: London.

4. SARAH, P. (1974). *Unpublished M.Phil Thesis.* University of London Institute of Education.

5. SWANWICK, K. (1968). *Popular Music and the Teacher.* Pergamon. and SWANWICK, K. (1975). 'A Music Curriculum Project Described and Evaluated'. *Music Teacher.* December, 1975.

6. SPENCER, P. (1976). *Pop Music and the School.* Vulliamy and Lee (Ed). Cambridge.

7. BURNETT, M. (1977). *Music Education Review.* Vol. 1. Burnett (Ed).

8. YOUNG, M. (1971). *Knowledge and Control.* Collier-Macmillan.

9. I.L.E.A. (1973). *Obscured Horizons: Music in Schools.*

10. VULLIAMY, G. (1976). *Pop Music and the School.* Cambridge Univ. Press.

11. LAWTON, D. (1975). *Class, Culture and the Curriculum.* Routledge and Kegan Paul.

12. SMALL, C. (1977). *Music – Society – Education.* John Calder, London.

13. HOLT, J. (1976). *Instead of Education.* Penguin.

14. BRUNER, J. (1972). *The Relevance of Education.* Penguin.

15. SHEPHERD, J. (1977). *Whose Music?* London.

16. ROSS, M. (1975). *Arts and the Adolescent.* Schools Council Working Paper 54. Evans/Methuen.

17. ROSS, M. (1978). *The Creative Arts.* Heinemann.

18. WOLLHEIM, R. (1968). *Art and its Objects.* Penguin.

BIBLIOGRAPHY

BANTOCK, G.H. (1967). *Education, Culture and the Emotions.* Faber.

BERLIOZ, H. translated (1970). *The Memoirs of Hector Berloiz.* Panther. CAIRNS, D.

BERLYNE, D.E. (1974). *Studies in the New Experimental Aesthetics.* Hemisphere Publications: USA.

BLACKING, J. (1976). *How Musical is Man?* Faber.

BLOOM, B.S. (Ed) (1956). *Taxonomy of Educational Objectives,* Book 2. Longmans, Green and Co: New York.

BRACE, G. (1970). *Music and the Secondary School Timetable.* Exeter University.

BRUNER, J. (1972). *The Relevance of Education.* Penguin.

BURNETT, M. (1977). *Music Education Review.* Vol. 1. Burnett (Ed).

BURT, C.L. (1962). Critical Notice: The Psychology of Creative Ability. In: Vernon, P.E. (Ed) *Creativity,* Penguin, 1970.

COOKE, D. (1959). *The Language of Music.* OUP.

COPLAND, A. (1952). *Music and Imagination.* Mentor Books.

DEPARTMENT OF EDUCATION AND SCIENCE (1970). *Creative Music in Schools.*

DEWEY, John (1934). *Arts as Experience.* Capricorn Books: New York, 1958.

ELLIOT, R.K. (1971). *Versions of Creativity.* Proceedings of the Philosophy of Education Society of Great Britain, Vol. V., No. 2, July 1971.

EMPSON, W. (1961). *Seven Types of Ambiguity.* London.

FERGUSON, D. (1960). *Music as Metaphor.* Greenwood Press: USA, 1973 and 1976.

FINDLAY, J.W. (1968). 'The Perspicuous and the Poignant: two aesthetic fundamentals'. In: Osborne (Ed) *Aesthetics in the Modern World*. Thames and Hudson.

FORSTER, E.M. *Two Cheers for Democracy*. Penguin Books.

GUILFORD, J.P. (1959). Traits of Creativity. In: Vernon P.E. (Ed) *Creativity*. Penguin, 1970.

HANSLICK, E. (1854). 'The Beautiful in Music'. Liberal Arts Press: New York, 1957.

HEAD, H. (1920). *Studies in Neurology*. Oxford.

HEGEL *Aesthetics*.

HINDEMITH (1952). *The Composer's World*. Harvard. 38ff.

HOLT, J. (1976). *Instead of Education*. Penguin.

HUDSON, L. (1966). The Question of Creativity. In: Vernon P.E. (Ed) *Creativity*. Penguin, 1970.

I.L.E.A. (1973). *Obscured Horizons: Music in Schools*.

KELLER, HANS (1970). 'Towards a theory of Music'. In: The *Listener*. 11 June 1970.

KOESTLER, A. (1949). *Insight and Outlook*. Macmillan: London.

KOESTLER, A. (1964). *The Act of Creation*. Pan Books.

LANGER, S. (1942). *Philosophy in a New Key*. Mentor Books: New York, 1951.

LAURENCE, I. (1977). 'The Composer's View of the Teacher'. In: *Psychology of Music*, Vol. 5, No. 2.

LAWTON, D. (1975). *Class, Culture and the Curriculum*. Routledge and Kegan Paul.

LEE, VERNON (1932). *Music and its Lovers*. Unwin.

McLAUGHLIN, T. (1970). *Music and Communication*. Faber.

MAGER, R.F. (1975, 1962). *Preparing Instructional Objectives*. Fearon Publishers: USA.

MANHATTANVILLE MUSIC CURRICULUM PROGRAM (1970). Media Materials Inc. Bardonia, N.Y.

MEYER, L.B. (1965). *Emotion and Meaning in Music*. Chicago.

MURDOCK, G. and PHELPS, G. (1973). *Mass Media and the Secondary School*. Schools Council.

PAYNTER, J. and ASTON, P. (1970). *Sound and Silence – Classroom Projects in Creative Music*. Cambridge.

PETERS, R.S. (1966). *Ethics and Education*. Allen and Unwin.

PETERS, R.S. (1968). *The Logola Symposium on Feeling and Emotions*.

PRING, R. (1973). *Curriculum Integration: the need for clarification*. The New Era. (54,3).

REID, L.A. (1969). *Meaning in the Arts*. London.

REIMER, B. (1970). *A Philosophy of Music Education*. Prentice-Hall: New Jersey.

ROGERS, C.R. (1954). 'Towards a Theory of Creativity'. In: Vernon P.E. (Ed) *Creativity*. Penguin, 1970.

ROSS, M. (1975). *Arts and the Adolescent*. Schools Council Working Paper 54. Evans/Methuen.

ROSS, M. (1978). *The Creative Arts*. Heinemann.

SARAH, P. (1974). *Unpublished M.Phil Thesis*. University of London Institute of Education.

SCHOOLS COUNCIL (1972). *Music and Integrated Studies in the Secondary School*.

SCHOPENHAUER *The World as Will and Idea*.

SELF, G. (1967). *New Sounds in Class – A Contemporary Approach to Music*. Universal: London.

SHEPHERD, J. (1977). *Whose Music?* London.

SINNOTT, E.W. (1959). 'The Creativeness of Life'. In: Vernon P.E. (Ed) *Creativity*. Penguin, 1970.

SMALL, C. (1977). *Music – Society – Education.* John Calder: London.

SPENCER, H. (1911). *Education.* Williams and Norgate.

SPENCER, P. (1976). *Pop Music in School.* Vulliamy and Lee (Ed). Cambridge.

STORR, A. (1972). *The Dynamics of Creation.* Pelican. 1976.

SWANWICK, K. (1973). *Musical Cognition and Aesthetic Response.* Bull. Brit. Psychol. Soc. 26.

SWANWICK, K. (1968). *Popular Music and the Teacher.* Pergamon.

SWANWICK, K. (1975). 'A Music Curriculum Project Described and Evaluated'. *Music Teacher.* December 1975.

TIPPETT, M. (1974). *Moving Into Aquarius.* Paladin.

VULLIAMY, G. (1976). *Pop Music in School.* Vulliamy and Lee (Ed). Cambridge.

WALLACH, M.A. and KOGAN, N. (1965). 'A New Look at the Creativity – Intelligence Distinction'. In: Vernon P.E. (Ed) *Creativity.* Penguin, 1970.

WALLAS, G. (1926). 'The Art of Thought'. In: Vernon P.E. (Ed) *Creativity.* Penguin, 1970.

WITKIN, R.W. (1974). *The Intelligence of Feeling.* Heinemann: London.

WOLLHEIM, R. (1968). *Art and its Objects.* Penguin.

YOUNG, M. (1971). *Knowledge and Control.* Collier-Macmillan.

YOUNG, P.T. (1961). *Motivation and Emotion.* New York.

Index

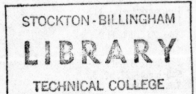